Creating Belonging in the Classroom

Creating Belonging in the Classroom

A practical guide to having brave and difficult conversations

Zahara Chowdhury

BLOOMSBURY EDUCATION
LONDON OXFORD NEW YORK NEW DELHI SYDNEY

BLOOMSBURY EDUCATION
Bloomsbury Publishing Plc
50 Bedford Square, London WC1B 3DP, UK
Bloomsbury Publishing Ireland Limited
29 Earlsfort Terrace, Dublin 2, D02 AY28, Ireland

BLOOMSBURY, BLOOMSBURY EDUCATION and the Diana logo are trademarks of Bloomsbury Publishing Plc

First published in the UK in 2025 by Bloomsbury Publishing Plc

This edition published in the UK in 2025 by Bloomsbury Publishing Plc

A catalogue record for this book is available from the British Library

ISBN: PB: 978-1-8019-9578-8; ePDF: 978-1-8019-9580-1; ePub: 978-1-8019-9577-1

2 4 6 8 10 9 7 5 3 1 (paperback)

Cover design by James Fraser

Typeset by Newgen Knowledge Works Pvt. Ltd., Chennai, India

Printed and bound in the UK by CPI Group (UK) Ltd., Croydon, CR0 4YY

For product safety related questions contact productsafety@bloomsbury.com

To find out more about our authors and books visit www.bloomsbury.com and sign up for our newsletters

To all of my ex-students.
I learned so much from every single one
of you, quite possibly more than you learned from me!
Thank you for making the classroom a safe space for me.

Contents

Acknowledgements

This book would not have been possible without the support, advice and encouragement of Rachel Smith, Dan Colquhoun, Frances Akinde and David Church.

Rachel Smith has not only been my manager and school leader; she has also been a career-long coach, mentor, advocate, ally, and friend (and work mum!). She has encouraged my success, confidence and development as a teacher and education leader. This book has only come to fruition with the opportunities she has given me over the last decade of my career. I hope every teacher is fortunate enough to have a leader like Rachel in the course of their careers.

I met Dan a few years ago, and his support, encouragement, and advocacy have enabled the case studies and student and staff voices in this book. Dan is a true ally, and the ways in which he has embedded and led inclusion and belonging in his school are commendable. Thank you so much, Dan, for all of your support!

A huge thanks to Frances and David for providing their time, expertise and advice for this book! I could not have written about LGBTQ+ inclusion, disability, neurodiversity and intersectional identities without their voices. Working in the DEI space can feel very isolating and vulnerable, and I am so grateful for colleagues, friends and the community I have found in professionals like Frances and David!

I would also like to thank Hannah Wilson, Nic Ponsford and Dr Penny Rabiger for their continued support, allyship and advocacy in this space. It's not easy working in the diversity and inclusion field, and it's really important to surround yourself with good people - I'm very grateful for their time and wisdom and for amplifying my work in the world of education.

Introduction

This book aims to support teachers with the language and tools they need to create genuine ***belonging*** in their classrooms – where every student feels they belong, and the classroom belongs to every student. While it cannot address every question about belonging, it offers practical starting points to help teachers navigate difficult conversations and build trusting relationships with their students. Through tips, examples and case studies, it provides an experience-based framework for developing a culture of belonging that can serve as an antidote to the misinformation surrounding prejudice, **diversity** and **inclusion** in public discourse.

Writing about belonging might seem idealistic rather than realistic. But my own experiences as both student and teacher have shown me how small moments in the classroom can have lasting impacts on a student's sense of belonging – for better or worse. These moments, seemingly insignificant at the time, can shape a student's educational journey and their understanding of their place in the world.

The meaning of belonging: my early student experience

The experience of belonging in school is rarely uniform and it is not necessarily something that students are consciously aware of *as* 'belonging'. Belonging is often a mix of positive connections with teachers, school staff, subjects, school trips, activities, school plays, and moments of exclusion too. In my experience, belonging, connection and inclusion are often *feelings* and, at school, the experiences we have in the classroom. My own story highlights the profound impact a teacher can have on a student's sense of belonging and how even a single comment can disrupt that connection.

I learned this lesson first-hand in my own English classroom. At first, reading and analysing Shakespeare's *Macbeth* felt like an impenetrable puzzle. No matter how hard I tried, the lines remained cryptic and the experience of sitting in lessons, reading and re-reading the playbooks, became an overwhelming experience to say the least. I remember watching my peers confidently making notes, raising their hands and making valid contributions, while I sat confused, feeling distinctly out of place. Mrs McGregor was well meaning, but I felt too intimidated to ask her any questions, believing I should just 'get' the text.

My next English teacher, Mrs Smith, was my favourite person at school, and English quickly became my favourite subject. I would stay behind during breaktime, eager to discuss everything from philosophy to politics, *EastEnders* to existentialism. Looking back now as a teacher myself, I marvel at her patience with my endless questions. Those conversations were more than just academic discussions – they were where I first felt I truly belonged in school. Someone understood me, listened to me, validated my thoughts. The classroom became my sanctuary, a place where I could be myself. I remember thinking, *this is so much fun. I belong here; someone understands me and listens to what I have to say.*

Everything changed when Mrs Smith started teaching me. She made it understandable. I remember how she would listen to all of our contributions, nod and say, 'That makes sense – and maybe Shakespeare is also…' – validating my thoughts even when they were tentative or slightly off base. Validation was important to me (and I'd be lying if I said it doesn't still matter), and she knew exactly how to bring out the best in me. Mrs Smith's approach was subtle but powerful, drawing out my potential through conversations and building a genuine relationship throughout my GCSE and A level years.

But it was this same teacher who unconsciously challenged my sense of belonging too. When I was studying for my GCSEs and couldn't push past a B grade, Mrs Smith explained it away with five simple words: 'It's because you're **EAL**.' I had never heard the acronym before, but I absorbed its meaning immediately – English as an Additional Language.

It wasn't said with malice; it was presented as a simple fact. But, as I reflect years later, I can see how that label became a barrier, a limitation I internalised as an impressionable young person; it was a moment where the idea of my 'difference' started to sink in. I would ask my white ones – not my Black or Asian ones – to teach me new words at break and lunchtime, not really knowing what I was asking, but desperately trying to 'learn more words'. As I write this, my own bias as a teenager is so present: why was I just asking my white friends and not my Black and Asian friends? The irony was that English had always been my primary language for communication.

This was the first time (in class) that I was consciously made aware of my differences in a limiting capacity. No unkindness had been intended, and in the moment, I hadn't yet processed the deeper implications. It was a passing, almost factual comment that felt so normalised and 'correct', but was wholly based on my appearance and 'background'. On reflection, it might have been said to help me improve, but I'm just not sure how.

That single exchange, brief as it was, planted a seed of self-doubt that grew far beyond that classroom. To this day, I still rely heavily on synonyms and have my writing triple-checked, haunted by the spectre of sounding 'too EAL'. It's shaped how I approach everything from job applications to writing this book. I am also very conscious of how uncomfortable it feels sharing this experience from over 20 years ago, revealing the long-term impact of classroom interactions too. Even when I started teaching, the prevailing belief was that the lack of high achievement in English among some students was primarily due to their EAL status.

Here's the complexity of belonging – this same teacher who unknowingly undermined my confidence also helped to build it in countless other ways. Mrs Smith encouraged me to apply to Oxford University, a path my family had never even considered. When I didn't get in, she insisted it was 'their loss'. When I chose to become a teacher, she welcomed me back to co-teach in the very classroom where I had once been her student. We co-taught Lawrence Ferlinghetti's *Two Scavengers in a Truck, Two Beautiful People in A Mercedes*. I miss her so much and I try to be what she was for me to all of my students. Her impact on my life was profound and largely positive. She will always be my favourite teacher.

This is why conversations about belonging are so nuanced. Students need compassion and forgiveness – and so do their teachers. We're all human, capable of both helping and hindering belonging, often without realising the impact of our words and actions.

Like every teacher, I've had days when creating a comfortable classroom feels almost impossible. Writing this book was not a decision I took lightly. Sharing personal experiences and offering practical advice requires vulnerability, especially when discussing something as complex as classroom belonging. I'm mindful that some colleagues might criticise these reflections as making assumptions about brilliant teachers with 'no evidence'. That's not my intention.

Instead, I hope this book encourages teachers to sit with some discomfort as we explore these issues together. Things are beginning to change, and space is opening up for more nuanced conversations about belonging. However, simply telling someone 'not to say it again' is no longer sufficient. We need to move beyond surface-level responses and engage with the underlying issues. When I trained to teach, we didn't talk about **microaggressions**. Any problematic exchange was handled with, at most, a quick reprimand at the end of class. We now know this approach isn't enough to address the subtle ways belonging can be undermined or strengthened in our classrooms.

This book offers practical tools, frameworks and examples to help teachers navigate these complexities with confidence. It's grounded in the reality that creating belonging isn't about perfection – it's about awareness, intention, and a willingness to keep learning and growing alongside our students. Through honest reflection and brave conversations, we can create classrooms where every student truly belongs.

Belonging for who?

In the UK, all individuals are protected by the Equality Act (2010), which defines nine 'protected characteristics': age, disability, gender reassignment, marriage or civil partnership status, pregnancy/maternity, race, religion, sex and sexual orientation. While we all have protected characteristics, some are more marginalised and discriminated against than others.

Throughout this book, I will often refer to 'underrepresented students'. When using this term, I'm referring to identities traditionally marginalised and underrepresented in classrooms and across the curriculum and historically. This includes:

- global majority students: students of colour, racialised as Black, Afro-Caribbean, Asian, South Asian, Arab and biracial heritage, who have been historically 'othered' in Western and European contexts;
- Gypsy, Traveller, Roma, Showmen and Boater students (GTRSB);
- **LGBTQ+** students: those identifying as lesbian, gay, bisexual, transgender or queer, with the '+' representing identities beyond **cisgender** and heteronormative experiences;
- disabled and neurodivergent students: those who may be categorised under **SEND** (special educational needs and disabilities) or have individual needs;
- students with religious backgrounds.

Additionally, this group contains refugees, students in care, those receiving free school meals, and students from working-class or disadvantaged socioeconomic backgrounds. You may be thinking, 'These students aren't necessarily underrepresented in my classroom.' However, the classroom and school environment – including curriculum, behaviour systems and **digital literacy** – may not fully represent or adapt to these students' needs.

As our schools, society and communities evolve, these demographics and identities will shift, continually redefining who is underrepresented, minoritised and marginalised in our classrooms. While this book aims to create a culture of belonging for every student, we must acknowledge that underrepresented students may feel less likely to belong in classrooms where they are a minority, or in lessons and curricula that do not reflect their experiences.

1 What is Belonging?

Belonging is both deeply personal and universally human. At its core, it's the feeling that we are fully seen and accepted for who we are, that we matter to others, and that we have a legitimate place in our community. In schools, belonging goes beyond simply being present in the classroom – it means *feeling* that you can authentically participate, contribute and thrive.

Think of belonging as a triangle, and its sides are labelled 'connection', 'representation' and 'voice'.

- **Connection** is about the relationships we build and maintain – with teachers, with peers, with the learning itself.
- **Representation** means seeing aspects of your identity and experience reflected in the curriculum, the classroom environment and the school community.
- **Voice** encompasses both the ability to speak up and the confidence that you will be heard when you do.

When students feel they belong, they aren't just physically present in the classroom – they're emotionally and intellectually present too. They feel safe enough to take academic risks, to ask questions, to make mistakes. They see their experiences and perspectives as valuable contributions to class discussions. They connect with the material being taught because they can see its relevance to their lives and futures.

However, belonging isn't a fixed state that we achieve once and for all. We won't feel that we belong *all* of the time, in every context and environment. The latter is often misunderstood. Belonging can also be a feeling developed by students over time, where they feel assured and confident enough within themselves to feel uncomfortable, to experience and overcome challenges in the classroom too. It's dynamic, shifting with context and circumstance.

Students can feel connected to their peers but disconnected from the curriculum. They might belong strongly in one moment and feel like an outsider in the next. This fluidity is crucial: belonging isn't about constant comfort, but about having the resilience to remain authentic across different environments. Understanding these nuances is crucial for teachers working to create a truly inclusive classroom.

The absence of belonging can manifest in various ways: from quiet disengagement to active resistance. Students who don't feel they belong might physically withdraw, participate minimally or act out. They might assimilate, **masking** aspects of their identity to fit in, or they might reject school culture entirely. These responses often reflect not just individual struggles but systemic barriers to belonging.

Creating genuine belonging isn't about lowering standards or avoiding challenge – quite the opposite. When students feel they truly belong, they're more likely to engage deeply with learning, persist through difficulties and achieve their full potential. This is why understanding and nurturing belonging is fundamental to effective teaching.

Elements of belonging

To translate this understanding into practice, we can focus on three key pillars that support belonging in the classroom: open communication, trust and safety, and shared passion. These pillars provide a practical framework for teachers to build environments where belonging can flourish, turning theoretical understanding into daily classroom practice. Let's examine each of these elements in detail:

- **Open communication** Fostering open and honest dialogue between students and teachers is crucial. This includes creating **safe spaces** for students to express their thoughts and feelings, actively listening to their perspectives, and engaging in respectful and meaningful conversations.
- **Trust and safety** Building trust and creating a safe and inclusive learning environment is paramount. This involves establishing clear and consistent classroom rules, promoting a culture of respect and kindness, addressing bullying and harassment promptly and effectively, and building positive relationships with students based on trust and mutual respect. Belonging does not mean abandoning boundaries, expectations or, dare I say it, necessary rules.
- **Shared passion** Cultivating a shared passion for learning is essential. This can be achieved by encouraging student engagement and curiosity through inquiry-based learning, creating opportunities for students to pursue their interests and passions, and celebrating student successes and achievements.

Throughout this book, we'll explore how belonging is built through daily interactions, curricular choices and classroom practices. We'll examine how open communication, trust and safety, and shared passion can work together to create environments where every student can thrive. Most importantly, we'll look at practical ways teachers can nurture belonging while navigating the complex realities of modern classrooms.

Belonging leads to long-lasting connection

Many of us have heard of the phrase 'fly the nest' for children as they grow into adults. Like the metaphor, when we're ready to spread our wings and embrace what the world has to offer, we fly and, hopefully, fly high. All being well, it is a time that children become young adults and are essentially able to fend for themselves.

However, while their sense of belonging shifts, the aim is to maintain a sense of connection with family, friends and community. Ideally, what a young adult takes forward isn't necessarily 'where they have come from', but rather the values and lessons they have learned to support them in order to flourish in the future.

A similar principle can be applied to students at school. Beyond learning facts, students develop critical thinking, problem-solving skills, and the ability to navigate complex workplace environments. If a student feels connected to your classroom and develops a strong sense of belonging, they're likely to internalise the deeper values you have nurtured there, such as kindness, respect and intellectual resilience.

I recall an A level class where we had developed a strong sense of connection. We had challenging conversations about the plays we were studying, but also about a range of other issues. During one particularly memorable lesson, I had a candid conversation about academic expectations and failure. The students were intensely focused on achieving top grades, and while they had the potential to, it was not something anyone could guarantee. In one lesson, I felt it important to offer a more nuanced perspective, explaining that while A and A* grades are achievable, other grades are also respectable and, realistically, top marks would not be the outcome for everyone. I emphasised that, while academic excellence was important, their potential wasn't solely defined by A* results.

The conversation was uncomfortable (some of those students remind me of that lesson to this day!). Years later, one student got back in touch and said they had just thought I was in a bad mood! Not everyone agreed, and some initially misunderstood my intent. Another student contacted me, acknowledging the discussion as 'harsh, but true'. Despite the initial discomfort, we maintained an environment where challenging conversations were possible. Students felt empowered to disagree, ask questions and engage critically.

Something else remarkable emerged: many students maintained connections long after the class, seeking advice and sharing achievements. To me, this demonstrates the true essence of belonging – a connection that transcends the immediate classroom experience and nurtures lifelong learning and mutual respect.

The difference belonging makes

While initial data on GCSE results may suggest that certain minority groups are achieving well, a closer look reveals significant disparities when factors like gender, socioeconomic status and special educational needs (SEN) are considered.

Student awards, attainment and overall wellbeing are all significantly impacted by factors beyond academic achievement, and a sense of belonging and connection is often underestimated in this regard. Award and attainment data, while useful for examination, is typically reported based on individual protected characteristics. For instance, a top-level look at 2022–2023 GCSE results reveals that Chinese students achieved the highest attainment 8 score (65.5), followed by Indian and Bangladeshi students (59.4 and 51.9, respectively). White Gypsy and Roma students had the lowest attainment 8 score (20.3), followed by Irish Traveller students and students of mixed white and Black Caribbean heritage.[1]

When we *only* look at these figures, we may find ourselves thinking, what's the problem? Minoritised students are doing well, achieving and succeeding, so they must be happy and feel a sense of belonging at school. However, when we take an intersectional approach and examine the attainment through the lens of gender and ethnicity, students receiving free school meals and with special educational needs, a different picture begins to form. This highlights the importance of examining attainment data through an intersectional lens to understand the true picture of student success and wellbeing. While national statistics are available, I encourage you to look at the intersectional, **lived experiences** of your students and student groups to see if you notice any patterns or trends emerging. These may challenge biases or confirm them. For example, in one school, there were surprised reactions upon analysing data, which revealed that Pakistani girls were making the highest rate of progress in a range of subjects. While staff were pleased, it was interesting to see biases being challenged, which may have previously influenced teaching, learning and relationships in the classroom.

The data also reveals that in every ethnic group, girls consistently outperform boys in attainment 8 scores. Boys are also disproportionately disciplined and diagnosed with learning disabilities, especially boys of colour. While women and girls have historically faced limited educational opportunities, they have made substantial progress in recent decades, unlike boys, whose academic progress has been slower.[2]

Several factors contribute to this gap, including traditional classroom structures that may not align with some boys' learning styles, and societal expectations that can influence their behaviour and engagement.

Addressing these disparities requires a multifaceted approach, including:

- **Challenging gender stereotypes:** this involves using diverse examples in teaching materials, encouraging all students to pursue their interests regardless of gender norms, and providing equal opportunities for participation and leadership.

---

[1]www.ethnicity-facts-figures.service.gov.uk/education-skills-and-training/11-to-16-years-old/gcse-results-attainment-8-for-children-aged-14-to-16-key-stage-4/latest

[2]It's important to note that while the conversation often centres around the term 'boys', it's crucial to acknowledge that gender identity is a spectrum, and this discussion should encompass all students, regardless of their gender identity.

- **Re-evaluating classroom practices:** shifting towards more inclusive and flexible teaching methods that cater to diverse learning styles.
- **Addressing systemic issues:** tackling issues of implicit bias and systemic racism that disproportionately impact students of colour.
- **Sharing the data with students:** presenting this information objectively and amplifying student voice to explore why they feel this may be. This approach to addressing the topic requires a high level of trust within the class, and can be effectively implemented through classroom discussions or focused, smaller student groups. This can be a powerful opportunity to learn alongside your students and develop a culture of belonging by amplifying student voices to explore their perspectives. It goes beyond traditional teaching, transforming data analysis into a collaborative process.

Students eligible for free school meals (often an indicator of socioeconomic disadvantage) score lower than those who are not. The average attainment 8 score for students with special educational needs is 28.1, compared to 50.0 for students without SEN. These disparities highlight potential barriers within schools, such as limited access to reasonable adjustments, resources, specialist funding and digital resources.

The COVID-19 pandemic amplified the need for internet access and digital tools for schools and students. It also exposed the stark reality for children from low-income families.[3]

We, as educators, understand too well the profound impact this can have on a student's sense of belonging in the classroom. The inability to access online homework or tasks, coupled with a lack of parental support with digital literacy, can lead to feelings of withdrawal, falling behind and alienation in our schools. Students may hesitate to ask for what they need, due to the misconception that everyone else is managing, leading to a sense of isolation. While these challenges often lie beyond a teacher's direct control, we can still foster a strong sense of belonging through simple acts of connection, such as engaging in conversations with students and actively seeking to understand their individual needs.

Teachers can foster a sense of belonging for students facing **digital exclusion** by offering flexible learning options, minimising reliance on online resources, and providing clear and concise instructions. You can also build strong relationships with families by communicating regularly and providing support to those facing digital barriers. Creating a supportive classroom community where students feel comfortable asking for help and collaborating with peers is crucial. Finally, advocating for increased

[3]www.cam.ac.uk/stories/digitaldivide#:~:text=The%20link%20between%20poverty%20and,compared%20to%20their%20wealthier%20peers.

access to technology and digital resources for all students is essential for addressing this issue effectively.

What do we need to belong *to*?

I recently spoke with Aisha Richards, the Founder and Director of Shades of Noir, an organisation that centres social justice pedagogy and the voices of marginalised students in Higher Education. When sharing the premise of this book with Aisha, she asked me to consider, 'Why do kids need to belong?' and it got me thinking:

- How do we frame belonging in the classroom?
- Do students have to 'fit in' to certain rules and expectations to belong in the classroom?
- What is it that students and staff belong *to*?

At an Inclusive Leadership conference I hosted at Buckinghamshire New University in collaboration with the Insignis Academy Trust, Aisha sparked a profound discussion about belonging. Ian Harper, the Commercial and Business Development Director, posed a pivotal question; not: *Do students belong in our settings?*, but rather: *Do our settings belong to our students?*

This challenging question demands a fundamental shift in our understanding of belonging. As teachers, of course, we want to create a culture of belonging, but along the way, we must also ask:

- Are students empowered in the classroom?
- Can they advocate for themselves and their peers?
- Do they feel able to challenge their teachers?
- Are they free to share their ideas?
- Do they feel enriched by the classroom, and equally important, can they enrich the classroom with their unique experiences and identities?

These questions don't have absolute answers, but they provide a framework for reflection. As classroom teachers or school leaders, you can:

- discuss these questions with colleagues
- evaluate curriculum materials
- examine your classroom environment.

The work of belonging is both simple and complex: it demands our curiosity, compassion, and commitment to seeing and valuing each student, fully and authentically.

When we examine secondary school curricula, SEND provisions, tightening school budgets and the impact of the cost-of-living crisis, particularly on Pakistani and Bangladeshi households, it becomes clear that a critical examination of the school environment is essential. We must ask: *Does every student feel they truly belong and are valued?*[4] To answer this question, schools can take concrete steps to foster a sense of belonging:

- **Curriculum:** ensure that the curriculum reflects all students' diverse experiences and perspectives. Include texts, historical figures and current events that represent a variety of cultures and backgrounds.
- **Teaching practices:** use inclusive teaching strategies that cater to different learning styles and abilities. Encourage critical thinking and open-minded discussions.
- **School culture:** promote a positive and supportive school climate where all students feel safe and respected. Address bullying and harassment, and celebrate diversity.
- **Support services:** provide adequate support services, such as counselling, tutoring and mentoring, to help students overcome barriers to learning.
- **Parental involvement:** engage with parents and guardians, particularly those from **marginalised communities**, to build strong partnerships and support student success.

You might be thinking, *how can I achieve this in my classroom while teaching for four to five hours a day, on top of planning, preparation and marking*? The simple answer is you cannot do all of this in isolation. Nurturing and sustaining a culture of belonging is a collaborative effort that requires the involvement of the entire school.

A whole-school endeavour

Creating a truly inclusive school environment that embraces Diversity, Equity, Inclusion, Justice and Belonging (DEIJB) is a complex and ongoing challenge.

---

[4]www.ethnicity-facts-figures.service.gov.uk/work-pay-and-benefits/pay-and-income/people-in-low-income-households/latest/ 31/07/2024

Why? Because nurturing a culture of belonging and inclusion goes beyond curriculum updates and adding holidays to the school calendar. It requires a fundamental shift in mindset and practice. For so many educators and students, especially those of us from **minoritised communities**, the traditional education system often feels like it doesn't fully reflect our lived experiences. Often when discussing educational interventions, such as addressing academic gaps or implementing support plans, the focus unintentionally shifts toward the deficiencies of individual students, particularly those from minoritised backgrounds. This can create a narrative that portrays these students as needing to be 'fixed' rather than recognising that it is the system itself that requires change. Minoritised students and those who may need adjustments to their learning experiences often become part of a **deficit narrative** within the educational system.

Fostering a sense of belonging requires a whole-school effort. While individual teachers can create welcoming and inclusive classrooms, a truly supportive school environment requires buy-in and action from the *entire* school community (and this is where it gets uncomfortable). If you are a senior leader reading this book, you could consider the following:

- How do existing school policies and practices align with the principles of belonging outlined in this book?
- Are there areas where there is a disconnect between the school's stated values and its actual practices?
- What are the barriers to implementing a more inclusive and equitable school culture?
- To gain valuable insights, you could form a working group with students, teachers, middle leaders, and other key stakeholders. This group can engage in a critical dialogue around the following questions:
  - Do you agree with the principles of belonging outlined in this book? If so, how are these principles currently reflected in our school's practices?
  - Where are we successful in fostering a sense of belonging for all students? Where are there areas for improvement?
  - What are the biggest barriers to creating a truly inclusive school culture?
  - What specific actions can we take to improve our school's inclusivity and foster a stronger sense of belonging for all students?

These questions will help centre a discussion about belonging at your school setting. They will help you to critically consider belonging and safety across classrooms in your school. They may also lead to some exciting and motivating discussions, but difficult discussions too.

Different perspectives on belonging

Be warned – belonging won't always feel like cloud nine. After speaking to several teachers in a range of school settings, I realised that belonging isn't about achieving some idealised state of happiness. In fact, school and work rarely provide such consistent feelings; it's not a set of ideal moments or a token.

Belonging is a deeply personal experience: every response reflects an individual's lived experience. What feels like belonging to one person might be completely different for another. Some students and staff may genuinely love school – it's where they feel safe and happy and they wouldn't think of being anywhere else. Others may be more indifferent, viewing school primarily as a place to learn and grow, make friends and navigate the world's complexities without really questioning it. However, for some students and staff, especially those from minoritised backgrounds, the experience of belonging can be significantly more challenging. They may face questioning, teasing, bullying and a lack of representation in the curriculum. They may feel like outsiders and struggle to find their place within the school community. These students see themselves as the odd ones out.

Teachers operate in extremely high-pressure environments with limited resources and time and school can become a place of isolation and anything but belonging. They navigate diverse, opinionated classrooms with young minds who have a range of different, and sometimes conflicting, lived experiences. As well as teaching Shakespeare, Pythagoras and the Richter scale, we are increasingly expected to address complex social and emotional issues, including race, religion, social justice and identity. While many teachers are eager to have these conversations, there is simply not enough time or space for meaningful discussion.

Equally, it's often assumed that teachers will have all the answers and can offer profound wisdom on every issue – that is a lot of pressure.

Managing classroom discussions is a part of teacher training, however, confronting, exploring and discussing our own biases while trying to manage our students comes only with experience and uncomfortable conversations.

Ultimately, this book aims to equip teachers with the tools to effectively manage difficult discussions and inclusive environments that recognise and value every student's unique experience.

2 The Challenges of Creating Belonging

As teachers, we operate within school systems that can inadvertently undermine our efforts to create inclusive classrooms. Whole-school policies – such as rigid behaviour frameworks, uniform regulations or disciplinary procedures – may conflict with nurturing positive student relationships. These systemic structures can create tension between institutional requirements and individual classroom dynamics.

Our own unconscious biases and prejudices complicate this task even further. However, by critically *understanding* the impact of microaggressions, prejudice and systemic barriers, we can strategically adjust policies, processes and classroom practices to foster genuine belonging.

The impact of microaggressions, prejudice and bias

For me and many underrepresented people, a lack of belonging profoundly impacts our experience. It manifests as **imposter syndrome**: a persistent fear of being exposed as a 'fraud', despite evidence of success and competence. This is often accompanied by feelings of unworthiness, shame and exhaustion. There's an ongoing need to fit in, which can lead to masking: the act of consciously or unconsciously concealing one's true self to gain acceptance.

As a teacher, I acknowledge my own unconscious biases. When starting at a new school, I began teaching a Sixth Form class midway through the year. A group of boys walked in, boisterous, talking and laughing. I felt unnerved – with the negative stereotypes of boys in hoodies in my mind, I automatically thought they were going to be a difficult bunch to teach. Within five minutes, a couple of them asked me how I was, said it was nice to meet me and asked about my weekend – challenging my initial assumptions.

I acknowledge now the impact these thoughts had on me and my students, but they were still able to begin nurturing a sense of belonging for me, as well as themselves. I recognise the experiences of students with underrepresented identities and the barriers they have to overcome.

The effects of prejudice, bias, and feeling like an outsider begin early, making classroom relationships incredibly powerful and important.

Assimilation and masking

Experiences of classroom bias have become so normalised (and internalised by students, parents and carers too) that they often pass by with no consequence. For example, minoritised students may feel invisible, and may feel the need to assimilate, to mask their identity and culture to fit in. This internalisation can manifest in various ways. Students might downplay or hide aspects of their **cultural capital**, like specific vocabulary or references, for fear of being seen as 'different'. They might avoid discussing their family's traditions, their home lives or holidays if they're different from everyone else's in the classroom. This could include feeling unable to talk about religious holidays like Eid or Diwali if most of their classmates celebrate Christmas, or not sharing stories about visiting family abroad.

Internalisation can deeply affect how students think about their own families, inviting friends to their homes (if this is an option) or feeling different in social settings. These feelings may manifest as embarrassment or shame, for example if their parents or carers don't speak fluent English, maybe avoiding bringing them into school events or conversations. Some students have to translate for their parents during parent–teacher events, whether through verbal language or sign language, carrying an additional emotional and communicative responsibility that creates significant personal strain. Even small things, such as how students choose to wear their uniform or if they know certain slang, can be influenced by this internalised pressure to conform. They might feel the need to wear the right brand of shoes or style their hair in a certain way. They might pretend to understand a meme they don't know rather than risk being seen as out of touch. Lately, teachers have noticed masking manifesting itself in relation to the cost-of-living crisis: students show up to school with empty lunch boxes and pretend to eat. This act of masking their reality highlights the intense pressure to fit in, which is an extremely difficult experience.

While not all of this is directly within the teachers' control, it's crucial that we, as educators, are aware of these dynamics. These internalised pressures can influence our teaching practices and interactions with students. For instance, a teacher might unconsciously assume a student with limited English proficiency also has limited academic ability, which can lead to lower expectations and fewer opportunities. Or, you might not consider the impact of assigning homework which requires internet access at home when not all students have this.

Masking is almost innate in minoritised groups – like a curated Instagram feed that looks shiny yet conceals mental exhaustion. Behind every seemingly perfect reel is a constant need to adapt to cultural capital experienced across the curriculum. With **Gen Z** and **Gen Alpha** mastering this adaptation, teachers must consciously recognise its complexity. Addressing masking requires intentional strategies:

- Representation across the curriculum can help students to see diverse lived experiences. By presenting varied narratives, teachers can invite students to share their responses and personal resonances.
- Simple check-ins – using a single word or emoji to express feelings – can provide insight into student experiences.

Observing how students interact during different activities offers valuable emotional context. Thoughtful, individual observations can reveal underlying experiences:

'I noticed you enjoyed leading group work. How do you feel about that?'

'You seem distracted today. Is everything OK?'

'I've noticed your work style seems different. Would you like to discuss it?'

These approaches develop naturally as trusting relationships grow, allowing more nuanced understanding of student experiences over time.

Whiteness/the 'norm'

This brings me to a complex social identity that many feel compelled to belong to, be accepted by, and be seen within: whiteness. I understand that this might feel uncomfortable and jarring to read. However, I ask that you sit with any discomfort in a collective effort to understand 'whiteness' as a social idea that impacts us all.

Understanding whiteness is key to recognising systemic racism and **privilege**. By acknowledging the advantages often linked to whiteness, we can identify and address societal inequalities. Defining whiteness isn't about labelling people or creating divisions but about recognising the power dynamics at play in society.

When talking to speaker and academic Barnaby Raine about this, he shared what the activist Ambalavaner Sivanandan writes: anti-racist work isn't about privileging certain groups over others, but creating a world that is better for everyone. This is precisely what we as teachers aim to do daily in our classrooms – and addressing whiteness helps us to achieve this goal.

What is whiteness?

When using the term *whiteness*, I don't necessarily mean white people. I don't mean your white friends, family, neighbours, students or colleagues. I don't mean you (if you are racialised as white). The idea of being 'white' is a social concept that's often seen as the default standard. It's tied to a system that privileges those who fit into this narrow category, creating significant barriers for people who don't fit the norm (people of the Global Majority, those with disabilities, or LGBTQ+ individuals) to feel like they truly belong. Even some people who are categorised as 'white' can feel marginalised if they don't fully fit the mould.

When we consider 'belonging' and the importance of fostering it in our schools, we must recognise that the systemic and institutional understanding of belonging and 'comfort' – the idea of 'fitting in' – is rooted in historical, patriarchal and colonial images of whiteness. This reflection on whiteness often conjures up associations with purity, innocence, health, goodness, superiority and righteousness. It can be associated with heteronormativity, ableism, power and privilege. While these connotations can be uncomfortable and controversial, it's clear that the traditional notion of 'fitting in' within schools often privileges certain groups. When we examine the stark reality of school exclusions, we see that students who don't conform to the dominant norms are disproportionately affected. Gypsies, Roma and Irish Traveller students, followed by biracial White and Black Caribbean and Black Caribbean students, experience the highest rates of permanent exclusion.[5] While these are top-level figures and of course it is important to interrogate the data, data can provide a starting point for discussions and questions about belonging in the classroom, particularly if we acknowledge that belonging is centred around a privileged position that students from marginalised groups are continuously (whether this be conscious or unconsciously) measured against.

Fitting into a system vs. belonging

Of course, as teachers, we want our students to feel seen, heard and valued in our classrooms. However, if we expect students to 'fit in' to a system and curriculum that doesn't necessarily *represent* our students, they can normalise or internalise feelings of **assimilation** and fitting in, as opposed to feelings of belonging.

Unfortunately, most teacher training or CPD still doesn't adequately address issues of bias, equality and **equity**. Instead, marginalised identities are categorised as 'other' and therefore, consciously or subconsciously, the aspirational achievements and expectations of certain students may be limited. Much of what we learn about adaptive teaching, learning and intervention is often framed by a deficit narrative: we're working to support (marginalised) students to pass, not to thrive and be ambitious, but to just about *pass*.

Inclusion and belonging are often seen or manifested as a way to 'fit in' and assimilate with the dominant identity or culture, to become more like the norm, rather than

---

[5] www.ethnicity-facts-figures.service.gov.uk/education-skills-and-training/absence-and-exclusions/permanent-exclusions/latest/ 23/09/2024

enabling and empowering individuals to be their authentic selves at school. Failure to 'fit in' sometimes leads to shame or feelings of embarrassment. In her book *Atlas of The Heart*, Brené Brown defines the feeling of shame as feeling defective and undeserving of love, belonging and social bonds. This can relate to students' experiences in the classroom and at school: if your identity is associated with stereotypes, bias or quite simply ignored, you can end up feeling ashamed, angry, rebellious. At one school, a Sixth Form student shared that she was ashamed of bringing in last night's leftovers for lunch because fellow students complained about the smell. Something that was normal for her was made to seem 'weird' and 'nasty' at school, causing feelings of embarrassment and shame and resulting in her changing her lunch options.

A student with ADHD once came to my office to ask for some advice on how to communicate with her teacher. She wanted to express that if she needs to get up and walk around, or briefly leave the classroom, it doesn't mean she intends to be disruptive; rather, it's her way of managing her ADHD. These additional thoughts that underrepresented students have can be exhausting. The constant effort to hide one's true identity can contribute to feelings of depression and isolation. Suppressing emotions and feelings can lead to frustration and conflict in relationships with family, friends and peers. The mental and emotional energy required to mask negatively impacts focus and concentration.

This may all seem minor, but microaggressions like these can lead to students suppressing or masking their identities, which can have a detrimental impact on their wellbeing, and on their school and home lives too.

Classrooms are built for fairly large audiences and often, policies and practices take a collective approach. While this is a rational and logical strategy, it is important to note that things like behaviour policies, uniform policies and curriculum choices can impact students in different ways, affecting how they feel in the classroom, and their sense of belonging and safety.

Personalised experiences

Supporting students with one-to-one mentoring and extra lessons are common forms of intervention in schools. This approach focuses on providing targeted and tailored support to help students succeed and thrive in their educational environment. As a former intervention coordinator, I witnessed the positive impact of these interventions first hand. It was a valuable, rewarding and impactful experience.

As a teacher, I believed I was doing all the right things to support my students, and while I am still an advocate for thoughtful and purposeful interventions, I am now also aware that these measures can easily become a temporary fix for a much bigger problem: a lack of representation and belonging in the school community.

This is because, while interventions certainly have a positive impact, they can reinforce the notion that minoritised groups need special help to succeed and 'fit in'; that they are inherently deficient. For the student in question this can also create a sense of dependency. All of this is somewhat paradoxical for teachers and educators like you and me, 'fighting the good fight': we know in the current system such interventions and strategies are necessary and positive, but we are also aware they are effectively sticking plasters for gaping wounds. As educators, we need to flip the narrative and work on healing and repairing these institutional wounds, not just the children who are affected as a result of them.

I was fortunate to join a dynamic and supportive English department, where I was responsible for developing and delivering targeted intervention sessions for Years 10 and 11. Guided by a brilliant deputy headteacher who firmly believed in the potential of every student, I worked closely with my colleagues to create a supportive and challenging learning environment. We emphasised student agency and instilled a belief in their ability to achieve at the highest level.

Through dedicated effort and collaborative teamwork, we saw remarkable results that year. The vast majority of students who participated in the intervention sessions achieved A or A* grades in their controlled assessments. These were students who had lost their drive and interest in English because they were disengaged, did not think they could succeed in the subject and had consistently achieved grades far below their ambitions and aspirations.

Equally, I am fully aware that it is almost impossible for any teacher to create an individualised and fully personalised experience for every single student, marginalised or not, in the public or private sector. The important point to remember is that we are working with our students to consciously create learning experiences that reflect their lived experiences too.

3 Starting with Ourselves

Here's the thing about creating belonging in our classrooms – it starts with us. Before diving into all the strategies and techniques, we need to take an honest look at ourselves. I know that might sound a bit daunting, but stick with me. This chapter is all about getting comfortable with being uncomfortable, and developing the tools we need to create spaces where every student can truly belong.

The beauty of our job – and yes, it really is a privilege – is that we can help students to navigate and overcome tough experiences. Through difficult and brave conversations (even when they make us squirm a bit), we can help to empower all students to be their best selves. Most importantly, we can help to create a world where prejudice and bias are called out confidently. Pretty amazing, right?

Understanding our own biases

Here's where it gets interesting (and maybe a bit uncomfortable). To create classroom cultures where students thrive, belong and succeed, as well as considering the intersectional identities of all our students (see Chapter 4), we need to face up to our own biases. I know, I know – nobody likes to think they're biased. But we all are, and that's OK as long as we're willing to work on it.

Let me introduce you to something that really helped me: Bobbie Harro's 'Cycle of Socialization'. This is a framework that helps us to understand where our beliefs come from and how they affect our teaching. Here's how we can use it:

1 **Spot those messages** Think about all the messages you've received about race, gender, class, sexual orientation – everything. Where did they come from? Family? TV? School?

> **TIP**
>
> Instead of saying 'Oh, society taught me XYZ', try to remember specific moments. Maybe it was something a parent said, or a scene from your favourite film growing up.

2 **Recognise the impact** Consider how these messages have shaped your worldview, beliefs and behaviours. How have they influenced your interactions with others? Do you hold unconscious biases or stereotypes? Have you ever caught yourself making assumptions about a student based on their background? Have you ever said or done something that might have been insensitive or discriminatory? (It's OK – we all have. The important thing is recognising it.)

3 **Challenge your assumptions** Once you've identified the messages and their impact, start to question them. Are these messages accurate? Are they fair and just? How do they contribute to inequality and oppression? When you encounter a stereotype or prejudice, ask yourself: *Is this really true? What evidence do I have to support this belief?* Often, you'll find those 'truths' you've always believed aren't so true after all.

4 **Make change happen** Use the insights gained from reflecting on the cycle to develop strategies for interrupting and disrupting the cycle of socialisation in your own life. Here's what you can do:

   - Read books and watch films that challenge your perspective.
   - Listen to people whose experiences are different from yours.
   - Speak up when you hear something that's not right.
   - Use your position to support marginalised students.
   - Keep reflecting and learning – this isn't a one-time process.

By using Harro's 'Cycle of Socialization' as a guide for self-reflection, we can gain a deeper understanding of our own biases and take steps to dismantle them. This is an ongoing process that asks you for ongoing effort and commitment. If you can, set aside time for regular self-reflection to examine your thoughts, feelings and behaviours. Be honest with yourself, and be willing to admit when you've made a mistake. But also, be patient with yourself: changing any kind of beliefs and behaviours takes time and effort. The aim is to keep unlearning, getting it 'right' and redefine the power balance of belonging. Self-reflection makes us better learners and better allies. Some people say this is idealistic, but I like to regard it as hopeful.

What is an ally?

Allies stand up for marginalised and vulnerable people. In the classroom, this means actively supporting students experiencing discrimination, exclusion or bullying based on their identity. We can be an ally in a proactive way, which includes all of the tips and thoughts in this book, from intervening during immediate instances of harm, creating inclusive classroom environments (see page 43) and ensuring resources, displays and interactions represent diverse experiences (page 45).

What can I do to ally with my students in the classroom?

Students facing adversity in your classroom will often feel isolated and hesitant to speak up. To create a culture of belonging where every student feels safe, we need to acknowledge and address the challenges, stigmas and inequality experienced by minoritised communities. We, as allies, must speak up and challenge inequality to let students know that they are seen, heard and supported in your classroom. This may be during class discussions by acknowledging and sharing different perspectives and encouraging students to reflect and consider different perspectives too.

TIP

Allying with marginalised communities is intrinsically linked to nurturing a sense of belonging in your classroom. We may not always get it right, but a commitment to learning and growth, and a willingness to acknowledge and address our mistakes, will help you to build bridges and break down barriers with marginalised groups.

Getting buy-in from your class

Consider collaborating with your students on a statement like the one below:

> *'We are all learning. I am confronting my biases and sharing my lived experiences, just like you. I recognise that as your teacher, I have a position of authority. I recognise that you will look to me for answers and guidance too. I will try to use this authority responsibly and respectfully to create a classroom environment that is safe and inclusive for everyone.*
>
> *Our class commitment: The intention is to create a safe and accepting environment, and be mutually respectful. Any form of discrimination, prejudice or unkindness will be addressed. We will continue to learn about our biases and be accountable for our actions and words. We understand that mistakes may happen, and when they do, we will commit to learning from them. If I say or do something that causes hurt or pain, I will acknowledge it, apologise sincerely, and be open to learning from the experience and we will all do this for one another too. We will actively seek out diverse perspectives and experiences to broaden our understanding, by reading, discussing and learning together using a diverse range of resources in and outside of the classroom.*

> *I value your perspectives and experiences. I will listen to your thoughts and ideas, even if they differ from my own. What we hear and learn is representative of the lived experience and may not be representative of everyone – and that is OK. We will create a space where all students feel empowered to share their experiences and perspectives, ask questions, and challenge ideas.'*

The appropriate level of detail and specificity will vary depending on your school's existing policies on diversity and inclusion. You might not have a formal diversity and inclusion policy; however, you can share the class statement with other teachers and leaders to begin nurturing a culture of belonging across the school. Try to involve students in the development of classroom practices and agreements – the goal is to create a statement that is authentic and meaningful to you all.

Embrace discomfort

Addressing challenging topics never really gets comfortable. Even after years as a teacher, manager, leader, EDI trainer, blogger and podcaster, my heart races and I feel a little unsure of myself. But here's what I've learned: that discomfort is actually a good thing. Students appreciate when we're real about feeling uncertain or nervous, not that we're always right. It shows them it's OK not to have all the answers; it is how they grow, learn and understand how to navigate the difficult and challenging situations that lie ahead for them too.

The most meaningful relationships I've built with students came from moments when I admitted I didn't know everything. It's about being genuine, not perfect.

Overcoming the fear factor

Something I hear all the time from teenagers and teachers alike is that a key reason for minimising or avoiding conversations and discussions that concern social justice, identity and discomfort is that they 'don't want to say the wrong thing'. This fear of messing up keeps so many of us from having important conversations. Teachers tell me they 'tiptoe' around challenging topics, worried about the repercussions. It's natural to feel this way, and stems from a desire to be liked, to avoid conflict, and maintain social harmony.

There are so many resources for adults navigating difficult conversations, from podcasts to books, by authors like Simon Sinek and Blair Imani. If we provide tools for students to overcome the fear factor and have difficult conversations, imagine how prepared they'll be for life beyond school and in the workplace.

Telling our students to overcome the fear factor is much easier said than done! Be intentional in letting students know they can come and talk to you if they are unsure about anything or worried about bringing it up in class. Create a safe, supportive environment. Reassure students it's always better to talk, and understand they might need time to feel comfortable. Offering this as a first step also reduces the fear of talking about something they are worried about in front of an audience.

- **Encourage students to prepare**: if a student wants to talk, or if they are curious about, a particular topic, ask them to prepare for it before they talk about it. This might involve:
    - writing down what they want to talk about
    - preparing specific questions
    - reviewing the class communication guidelines to remind them to be respectful and responsible with their use of language
    - checking with you when the best time might be to talk. Is it at the end of the lesson? Does it need to be scheduled for a specific time in the week? Or, is it better discussed at an extracurricular club set up for these conversations?
- **Encourage precise language:** a conversation about social justice can be overwhelming and wide-ranging. Instead of broad, potentially judgmental statements, guide students to ask specific, respectful questions. Try to replace vague comments with clear, focused inquiries and transform general statements into specific, curiosity-driven questions.
- **Sentence starters:** it can help to provide conversation guidance and sentence starters.

    'I want to describe/explain something I read/saw, and I'll explain it carefully.'

    'This is a challenging topic, but important for us to discuss.'

    'I've been thinking about [lesson/resource] and have some thoughts.'

    'I'm unsure about [...] and would like help understanding.'

    'This is what I think. What do others think?'
- **Response prompts:**

    'What do you think about...?'

    'I'm not sure... What's your perspective?'

    'Some might feel... and that's OK.'

By providing structured support, teachers can help students to develop more nuanced communication skills.

> **TIP**
>
> Before speaking, ask yourself (and ask students to ask themselves): *Are my intentions genuine? Am I trying to understand or help?* Start with smaller conversations and gradually increase the complexity of the topics you discuss.

Creating a culture of belonging for neurodiverse students

Creating a sense of belonging isn't a passive process – it demands intentional, strategic design, as Frances Akinde, a seasoned headteacher and education consultant, powerfully articulates. She agrees that language matters, but what terminology should schools use? Is SEND OK? Should we use **neurodiversity** or neurodivergence? I have often found that teachers say nothing at all because they 'don't know what to say'. Akinde's advice is to respect the terms that students and their families prefer. Consistent use of terms like 'neurodiversity' and 'neurodivergence' can help emphasise the diversity of our brains but talking about these terms always starts a lively discussion. It's crucial to avoid using language that carries negative connotations. Terms that frame neurodiversity as a 'disorder' or 'deficit' can be stigmatising and harmful. In recent years, there has been a significant shift away from the medical model, which often viewed neurodiversity as a condition that needs to be 'fixed' or 'cured'. This shift recognises that neurodiversity is a natural variation in human cognition and that many neurodivergent individuals possess unique strengths and talents.

While it is not always the case, neurodivergent students often possess exceptional creativity, innovative thinking, and strong problem-solving skills. Autism can lead to heightened attention to detail, while dyslexia can foster strong visual-spatial skills. Some neurodivergent individuals often possess strong analytical skills, which can be a valuable asset in collaborative learning environments. Having neurodiverse students in your classroom will bring unique perspectives and ways of enriching discussions and challenging conventional thinking.

While neurodiversity brings a wealth of strengths to the classroom, it's important to acknowledge the challenges teachers may face in accommodating the diverse needs of neurodivergent learners within a traditional classroom environment – and this is not the fault of the teacher. Fixed timetables, standardised assessments, and a focus on uniform learning objectives can create barriers for some students. Students with sensory sensitivities may find the noise and sensory stimulation of a typical classroom environment overwhelming, while others may struggle with the fast pace and rigid structure of traditional teaching methods. Recognising these challenges and proactively addressing them where possible, by adapting or changing instructions, flexible learning environments and appropriate support systems, is crucial for creating a supportive learning environment.

Creating a culture of belonging for the LGBTQ+ community

LGBTQ+ youth face unique challenges in school, including higher rates of bullying, harassment and discrimination. For so many years, comments like 'That's so gay!' have been 'normalised' and disregarded as banter. There are others, too, that impact different groups of people: 'Man up!', 'Stop acting like a girl', 'Boys don't cry', 'You're so butch'...and more. So many of us have internalised and 'normalised' these comments. Whether intentional or not, by doing this, we are also responsible for creating unsafe spaces for marginalised communities. All educators have a role to play in creating a safe and inclusive environment for students. Demonstrating **allyship** is more important than ever, and we must address all comments and actions that will affect LGBTQ+ students' belonging and safety. It's also important to acknowledge that the experiences of LGBTQ+ individuals intersect with other identities such as race, ethnicity, class and disability.

Solidarity with LGBTQ+ youth requires more than just tolerance; it demands active efforts to dismantle systems of oppression and create an inclusive school environment. This involves challenging homophobia and transphobia, and celebrating LGBTQ+ history and culture.

Building empathy and compassion

To be an ally, have challenging discussions in the classroom and create a classroom culture of belonging and safety for everyone in it. At the same time, it's important that we practise empathy and compassion in the classroom too.

What is empathy?

Now, we've mentioned being patient with yourself; let's talk about empathy and compassion – and no, they're not the same thing! Within the context of the classroom, empathy is listening to someone's story, and understanding their perspective, even when it is different from your own. It's about acknowledging their unique experience without projecting our own assumptions onto them. It's not about fixing or correcting – it's about understanding.

I love how Brené Brown explains it in *Atlas of the Heart* (an absolutely great read, by the way!): 'We need to dispel the myth that empathy is "walking in someone else's shoes." Rather than walking in your shoes, I need to learn how to listen to the story you tell about what it's like in your shoes and believe you even when it doesn't match my experiences ' Her emphasis on active listening and really validating another person's perspective is crucial for building meaningful connections. This way of thinking is so apt for the classroom as it encourages students and staff to listen, acknowledge and feel what others are saying and experiencing.

Engaging in open and honest dialogue with students, actively listening to their perspectives, and creating a safe space for them to express themselves are essential for building those strong relationships and fostering a sense of belonging. When students feel safe sharing their thoughts and feelings, even when those are uncomfortable or challenging, it allows for genuine learning and growth. It also helps to develop critical thinking skills, challenge assumptions, and build empathy. To encourage this in the classroom, teachers can model empathetic responses. Here are some phrases I've found helpful:

'I hadn't thought about it like that before.'

'That's an interesting perspective.'

'I didn't realise that's how it feels for you and it's really good to know.'

'I don't fully understand yet but it would be good to learn more about it from you. Can you tell me more?'

Here are some phrases that students can use and you can perhaps display in your classroom or during lessons too:

'I can see why you feel that way.'

'That must have been really difficult.'

'I appreciate you being honest.'

'I'm trying to understand your point of view better.'

'I can see how that would be frustrating.'

'It sounds like you're feeling [emotion]. Is that right?'

'I'm here to listen if you want to talk about it.'

We can also explicitly teach empathetic communication skills to our students. This can be through class discussions, role-playing activities, and providing a list of empathetic phrases they can use in their interactions with peers.

Use the phrase banks in this chapter to help you respond to students when you feel you are not in a position to fully understand their experiences.

What empathy is *not*

It is important to note that attempting to correct, 'fix' or persuade students to see things from a mainstream perspective is not empathy in the classroom (or elsewhere!). Here are real examples that have come from teachers who have tried to resolve a challenging discussion:

1 *'We know Black Lives Matter, but all lives matter too.'*

2 *'We understand individuals practise different faiths, but we try to keep faith out of this classroom in order for everyone to be and feel safe and learn equally.'*

3 *'Of course, we must acknowledge every individual identity and gender, however, it is important to understand that people can make mistakes too.'*

How might the sentences above cause a lack of belonging? Here's how we can make the statements more genuinely inclusive:

1 *'It's important to understand that the statement 'Black Lives Matter' acknowledges a crucial point: throughout history, systemic inequalities have unfortunately devalued Black lives. This recognition is not about denying the value of any life but about highlighting the urgent need to address the ongoing impact of these historical injustices. By emphasising that Black Lives Matter, we strive towards a society where everyone has the opportunity to thrive and where true equality and justice prevail.'*

This reply focuses on a positive goal: creating a more equitable society for all, emphasising the importance of acknowledging history without being accusatory and reframing the statement. Instead of 'ignores historical context', it emphasises the importance of understanding historical context.

2 *'Faith is a core part of individual identities, not an additional feature. Some of us have been raised in households where faith shapes our environment, actions and values. Whether we practise a faith or not, we share fundamental principles like kindness, respect and patience. By understanding more about each other, including our faiths and belief systems, we create a culture of belonging – exactly as we committed to in our class statement.'*

This reply centres an understanding of faith and belonging for all in the classroom as the end goal. It does not aim to shut down any discussion; rather it aims to explain the importance of faith for individuals and our responsibility to respect individual identities.

3 *'Gender and sexual orientation are part of individual identities. They are also personal and private and we must respect the privacy of every individual. In the same way there may be several elements of our identities we do not want to share, there is no obligation for someone to share information about their gender or sexual orientation either. Of course, misgendering is a horrible experience and I want everyone to know that you are safe to share information about how you would like to identify and be referred to in this classroom. If we get something wrong, please tell us and we will do our best and make sure we avoid mistakes in the future.'*

This reply emphasises that there is no expectation for people to share their gender, **pronouns** or sexual orientation. It centres respect and safety, while letting members of the LGBTQ+ community know that we will keep ourselves accountable too.

'I KNOW WHAT YOU MEAN, BUT...'

Here's a challenging question: do you actually 'know what they mean' or do you just want to get your point across, without acknowledging theirs? Questions like this one ensure that students (and staff) are aware of the need for them to be respectful and remind them to adopt an empathetic and compassionate approach. Sometimes, being direct is best too!

Ending a discussion with 'but' or another perspective, like those real-life examples above, diminishes the impact of the initial point and make students or staff feel that, while they were given space to talk about their experiences and feelings, they were not really understood or listened to. Creating a safe space with empathy involves active listening and centring the voices of marginalised individuals; it is not a place to correct or fix the perspectives you are hearing, which leads to people feeling overshadowed or dismissed.

The goal is to create a sense of belonging where everyone feels heard and seen. That goes beyond simply ensuring everyone has a chance to speak; it's about amplifying the voices of marginalised individuals and ensuring their experiences are valued and considered.

In practice, this may look like:

- facilitating a discussion where you consciously introduce diverse, differing opinions:

  'We're going to hear a range of opinions from the class. It's important that we listen to everyone in the first instance.'

- adding some prompts to reflect:

  'Which views resonate with you?'

  'Are there experiences we haven't considered?'

  'Let's agree to disagree: how do we feel about what's been said?'

  'Remember, you can't say "but"!'

TIP

Remember, while these discussions and topics are challenging, it is not necessary that you need to reach a general or equal consensus in the classroom. You can even start a discussion or steer a discussion in this direction too:

> *'It's not necessary that we will all agree with each other and we also don't need to convince one another about different perspectives. The point is to listen to one another and gain an understanding of different perspectives.'*

This can help to set an expectation about the nature of the discussion from the outset.

Compassion: the next step

Compassion is different. As Brené Brown puts it, compassion is about recognising our shared humanity and treating everyone with loving kindness. But here's the tricky part – this can feel at odds with our teacher training. We're taught to solve problems and get results, right?

Sometimes, the most compassionate thing we can do is just listen. Let students talk. Listen (and listen intently). Create that safe space where students can share their feelings. Ask them what they need instead of assuming we know. Compassion will come as we build trusting relationships in the classroom, continue to address challenging topics and conversations, amplify marginalised and hidden student voices so that students know your classroom, and your school is a place they are seen, heard and understood.

Sometimes being compassionate means supporting and listening to our students when they are struggling, even if we can't fix their problems. We can ally with our students (see page 23).

Compassion in the context of the classroom means showing support and understanding for students who are struggling or feeling frustrated due to their lived experiences. Here are a few ways teachers can demonstrate compassion:

- **Acknowledge and address microaggressions:** even if you don't witness them directly, acknowledge the impact of microaggressions on students. Use school-wide reporting systems for reporting and addressing bullying or discriminatory behaviour.
- **Create a safe space for diverse beliefs:** recognise the frustrations a student feels when they are unable to talk about their beliefs or faith from fear of prejudice or stereotyping. Create a space to enable these conversations to occur respectfully. This may include addressing opportunities on the curriculum to enable these discussions (covered in more depth in Chapter 11).
- **Support neurodivergent students:** recognise the barriers they face in accessing resources and navigating different exam styles. Make space to listen to these students about what they need and request reasonable accommodations to support their learning. **Reverse mentoring** (Chapter 13) could also be useful here.

The *actions* above are not solutions. They come from you listening to students and developing a culture of belonging where students feel seen and heard. The actions are a result of listening to students without preconceptions or judgements, and are effectively a result of compassion and empathy in the classroom.

It's important to remember that allyship is an ongoing process. While you can ally and support students in the classroom, there may be concerns that still need escalating according to your school's behaviour policy and code of conduct.

- **Escalating concerns:** if a complaint is not addressed, escalate the issue through appropriate channels within the school or institution.
- **Documenting concerns:** keep records of all interactions and attempts to address the issue.
- **Seeking support from colleagues:** connect with other educators who can offer support and guidance.

While it can be frustrating when initial efforts don't yield immediate results, it's important to remember that creating a more inclusive and equitable learning environment takes sustained effort and perseverance.

Learning and growing together

Here's something that took me way too long to figure out: empathy and compassion are not things we're born with – they're skills we need to practise. Just like reading and writing, they need to be learned and developed.

Sure, some people might seem naturally more empathetic than others. It's important to acknowledge that they're not innate qualities and that not everyone possesses them to the same degree. Teachers and staff can actively develop these crucial skills through intentional professional growth. This involves deep self-reflection, reading about diverse lived experiences, and engaging in meaningful conversations. The most useful ways to do this are reading about different lived experiences (see the suggested reading list at the end of this book) and engaging in meaningful conversations with one another. I often use Big Talk cards, founded by Fulbright Scholar Kalina Silverman, which inspire profound dialogue. These are by far the best ways to strengthen your empathy skills. These approaches go beyond traditional professional development, encouraging a more nuanced, empathetic approach to teaching and interaction.

Phrases to use in an empathetic classroom

To create an empathetic classroom, you might say:

- *'I am aware X has happened. I'm here to listen as and when and if you need.'*
- *'I don't know very much about X, and I'd really like to hear your perspective and learn from your experience. Would it be OK for you to share it with me?'*
- *'I know I don't always get it right, which might not be what you're looking for. I'm here to listen, learn and understand more about this so I can do better.'*
- *'OK, I hear you, and I would like to ask, how can we make it better for you? What sorts of things would you like to see? I'd love to hear your thoughts so we can take them forwards and see what we can do.'*

You can apply these statements to different situations. They aim to present a state of listening, open-mindedness and compassion. You can let students know that while you may not have a solution or be able to resolve the problem entirely, you can help by listening and advising on the next steps, depending on the situation. When teachers are attempting to engage in a discussion with students who feel disempowered and angry, or even vulnerable and scared, it helps if you and the students approach these discussions with clarity and transparency.

Moving forward

As we wrap up this chapter, remember – this work isn't about being perfect. It's about being willing to learn, grow, and sometimes mess up. Every step you take, to practise self-awareness and reflection, the skills of empathy and challenging conversations, is a step towards creating a classroom where every student can truly belong.

FINAL THOUGHT

Start small, be genuine, and keep learning. Your students will appreciate your authenticity more than your perfection. For now, maybe pick one area where you'd like to grow. It may be reading this book, reading one of the recommended reads at the end of this book, editing a part of your curriculum map to be more representative of your students and brushing up on your knowledge, or it may be having ten-minute discussions with your classes, once a week, to understand what belonging means to them? All of these micro-steps can have a macro impact.

4 Understanding Individual, Intersectional Lives

This chapter explores the complicated nature of belonging in the classroom. We start by acknowledging the limitations of focusing solely on individual 'protected characteristics' (race, religion, disability, neurodiversity, gender and sexual orientation). While these are important considerations, they rarely exist in isolation (see Harro's 'Cycle of Socialization' in Chapter 3 and Crenshaw's work on intersectionality). Instead, our students' identities and our own are complex and interwoven, forming unique and multifaceted experiences.

Protected characteristics: taking an intersectional approach

When I first thought about writing this book, I planned to write a nice, neat chapter for each minoritised 'protected characteristic': a range of themes that impact belonging in the classroom, including race and **anti-racism**, religion, disability, neurodiversity, masculinity, and LGBTQ+ issues, all of which fall under the broader umbrella of diversity, inclusion and equity. But that structure has proven extremely difficult to put down on paper!

Firstly, it's because each protected characteristic deserves a whole book in its own right: there is so much to say, and I'm am not an expert in any of them (rather an expert learner). Secondly, when thinking about *belonging*, I found it impossible to focus on each element of an identity in isolation. Belonging is so personal, mutable and ever-growing. For students in the midst of their teenage years, it's even more multifaceted and they cannot be removed or dissected from different parts of their identities.

So instead, I've taken an intersectional approach, with case studies, student and teacher voices to capture just how varied and wholesome belonging is and can be in school.[6] We can't fully understand a student's experience by examining their race, without also thinking about their gender or socioeconomic status. It's important to understand that within our different identities, some aspects can lead to feeling

[6]The term 'intersectionality' was originally coined by Kimberlé Crenshaw in 1989 to explain the inequality and oppression faced by African-American Women. Read Crenshaw's journal article, 'Mapping the Margins: Intersectionality, Identity Politics, and Violence against Women of Color' (1991), to learn more about intersectionality.

marginalised or excluded more than others. For example, members of the LGBTQ+ community often feel underrepresented or undervalued in classrooms due to their **gender identity** or sexual orientation. Some students may feel stereotyped and excluded because of their race rather than their gender. In schools that are transitioning from single-sex to co-educational settings, or single-sex schools with a co-ed Sixth Form, students whose gender identity is in the minority may feel particularly uncomfortable or excluded. Recognising this complexity is crucial for creating a properly supportive learning environment.

Acknowledging inequalities

Beyond individual identities, we have to acknowledge the systemic and structural inequalities in our education system. These are the deeply ingrained, often invisible and unexplained (or under-researched) ways that the UK education system's policies, practices and structures create and perpetuate disadvantage for certain groups of students.

- **Systemic** This highlights that the inequalities are not isolated incidents or the result of individual biases. They are embedded in the fabric of the education system as a whole from awarding gaps, curriculum content and design, to recruitment and retention, particularly of marginalised and minoritised staff.
- **Structural** This emphasises how these inequalities are built into the structure of the system, such as:
  - **Funding inequalities:** unequal distribution of resources across schools, often favouring well-off areas.
  - **Racial and socioeconomic segregation:** students from marginalised communities are often concentrated in under-resourced schools.
  - **Implicit bias:** unconscious biases held by teachers and other educators impact student expectations and opportunities (see Chapter 3 for more information on unconscious bias and socialisation).
  - **Standardised testing:** standardised tests don't always accurately reflect the abilities and potential of every student, particularly those from marginalised backgrounds or who are neurodiverse.
  - **Lack of diversity among educators:** a lack of diversity among teachers contributes to a lack of cultural understanding and limits students' access to role models.

Both systemic and structural inequalities overlap to form significant barriers to educational success. They can lead to differences in academic achievement, in access to higher education and, ultimately, to life outcomes. In 2023, The Office for Students reported that the degree outcomes for full-time Black students were 'consistently lower' than the outcomes for full-time White students over a six-year period.[7] These disparities are consistent for disabled students and other minoritised students too.

Addressing these disparities requires a multifaceted approach that involves:

- **Reforming education policies: to ensure unbiased funding and resource distribution across schools.**

  Teachers can advocate for their school to receive fair funding, ensuring all students have access to necessary resources like books, technology and extracurricular activities. We can participate in school improvement plans and make sure we proactively communicate the needs of our students to school leaders and governing bodies. Within the constraints of their budget, senior staff can seek out community partnerships for donations, and apply for grants to supplement school funding. Several workplaces collaborate with schools and education providers, and can help with access to career advice, mentoring, work experience and more, particularly for marginalised and minoritised students to gain better access and experience to the world of work.

- **Diversifying the teaching workforce: to create a more representative and culturally responsive education system.**

  There are some brilliant charities and programmes that support representation and diversity in teaching, such as the BAMEEd Network, The Anti-racist Schools Award, the BAMEEd SEND Network, Black Men Teach, DiverseEd, Pride and Progress, The Global Equality Collective and, most recently, a network I co-founded with educators Yamina Bibi and Sejal Patel, The South Asian Educators' Network.

  These networks are beneficial for staff and students. They provide a supportive network for education staff from racially minoritised communities and they can support schools looking for positive role models and representation for their students too.

  Of course, there is a long way to go; if you come from an underrepresented background, you could serve as a positive role model for students and perhaps create a professional network too. All teachers can support initiatives to increase the diversity of the teaching workforce and encourage students from different backgrounds to consider teaching as a career.

[7] Office for Students (OfS) Access and participation data and consultation findings | Advance HE

- **Addressing implicit bias: through professional development and training for educators.**

  We should have high expectations for every student, regardless of their background, and provide support and encouragement to help them achieve their full potential. Tools like Bobbie Harro's 'Cycle of Socialization' and Leeds Beckett University's Anti-racist Schools Award programme provide structured approaches to addressing institutional bias. By creating consistent opportunities for staff training and development, schools can become more accountable and cultivate a more equitable culture.

- **Re-evaluating assessment practices:** to ensure that all students have an opportunity to demonstrate their full potential.

  Advocate for a more holistic approach to assessment that includes a variety of methods, such as project-based learning, portfolios and presentations including spoken assessments, to provide a more accurate picture of student learning. Adapting assessment styles can be particularly beneficial for neurodivergent students. We can also focus on developing students' critical thinking and problem-solving skills, which are essential for success beyond standardised tests.

- **Empowering student voice: to ensure that the voices and experiences of marginalised students are heard and considered in decision-making processes.**
  See Chapter 13 on reverse mentoring.

Talking 'with' not 'at' – wise interventions

In his book, *Belonging*, Professor Geoffrey L. Cohen emphasises the importance of **wise interventions**.[8] These are small but impactful actions that can significantly enhance student wellbeing and academic success. There are so many examples of wise interventions where teachers have crafted situations, sometimes unknowingly, to learn about student interests, hobbies, views and opinions, outside the realms of exam rubrics.

For example, based on Cohen's concept of 'wise interventions' a teacher might:

- Create an 'empowerment box' where students can drop in a note or idea that can make learning and success empowering for them. This can also be anonymous so that students feel safe and not vulnerable.

---

[8] G. L. Cohen, *Belonging: The Science of Creating Connection and Building Trust*, New York, W. W. Norton & Company, 2022, pp. 212–40.

- Ensure resources are representative of the students they teach so that students identify with what they are learning.
- Start a lesson with a positive news story, a clip from a podcast or article linked to the success of students in the classroom. Steven Bartlett's podcast, *Diary of a CEO*, along with Elizabeth Day's podcast, *How to Fail*, include some brilliant gems that can, over time, inspire and harness a sense of belonging and confidence in all students so that they know your classroom is one where they can absolutely thrive.
- On rotation, check in with different students to see how they're getting on and if there is anything they need in lessons. This is minor and something we probably do all the time, however, the more we do it, the more likely students are to feel confident speaking to us as their educators about what they need.

Wise interventions and creating a culture of positive wellbeing can be trial and error until you find the interventions that work for your students in your lessons – and that's absolutely fine. They will be unique to your teaching style and your students' learning styles, but they may still be something you can share with fellow teachers.

Wise interventions transform classroom belonging from a passive concept to an active, meaningful experience. It's not just about representation, but creating an environment where students know their presence is vital, necessary, and would be genuinely missed. By amplifying student voices, ensuring curriculum representation, and implementing thoughtful interventions, we increase students' connection, confidence and, ultimately, their engagement and academic success.

I once taught a student A level English Literature and it was *not* their first choice. They didn't even meet the minimum requirements for A level English Literature; however, overall, they met the minimum requirements for Sixth Form. They had wanted to choose a very different subject from English, but it wasn't offered at the Sixth Form and their parents wanted them to remain at the school.

In the first few weeks, this particular student was so quiet – every time I looked over, they looked almost scared. A couple of weeks in, during the 'getting to know each other' phase, I would always check in to make sure they were OK, but as a teacher, you also don't want to come across as overbearing or worse, patronising.

Somehow, through a few conversations about their interests and intentionally letting them know they could see me at breaktimes and lunchtimes with any questions, the student started to open up. They had a great sense of humour and were much loved by their peers for this and their general charisma. I knew they were working as hard as they could and that was all I could ask for as their teacher. I also intentionally seated them with students I knew they'd feel safe with who would support them as and when necessary. We also had conversations where they informed me they were doing everything they could to make their mum proud, and I did my best to reassure them, their mum was *absolutely* proud of them.

Ultimately, they passed A level English Literature and I was so proud of them. The interventions this student needed the most were emphasising their strengths, the minor check-ins and the reassurance that help is always available if required.

It may sound simple, and as teachers, we have so many examples of moments where we have supported students in the most straightforward manner – things we wouldn't even call interventions. But these 'wise interventions' can make all the difference to a student's sense of belonging.

I know first-hand that schools are high-pressure environments, particularly when it comes to attainment. It's no secret that teaching a full day of classes is exhausting. Throw in the constant buzz of social media and the added pressures of supporting marginalised students, and it can feel like there's always something beyond our control. My conversations with other teachers have revealed that seemingly small interventions can have a profound impact on student belonging, achievement and overall wellbeing.

As we saw above, wise interventions go beyond simply providing information or setting rules; instead, they focus on how students interpret their experiences and themselves within the learning environment. For example, instead of simply telling a student they 'need to try harder', a teacher could employ a 'wise intervention' by:

- **Prompting new meanings:** instead of focusing solely on a grade, the teacher could guide the student to reflect on the effort invested, identify areas for improvement and explore alternative learning strategies.
- **Encouraging action:** you could encourage the student to explain their learning process to a peer, which can help them to solidify their understanding and build confidence in their own learning.
- **Direct labelling:** instead of emphasising the student's 'weaknesses', the teacher could highlight their strengths and potential for growth, emphasising their 'growth mindset' and capacity for improvement.

These seemingly small interventions can have such a profound impact. By addressing the basic psychological factors that contribute to students' struggles (such as feelings of inadequacy, fear of failure or lack of belonging), we can create a more supportive and empowering learning environment. These wise interventions are not about 'fixing' students but about empowering them to navigate challenges, develop resilience and, ultimately, to achieve their full potential. For me and many teachers, wise interventions also manifest as the candid conversations that run on into lunchtime, breaktime, and sometimes start in form time.

Conversations outside the classroom

Fostering belonging extends beyond the classroom. Extracurricular clubs, group discussions and even conversations in the corridors when you see a student who looks a little troubled or needs help – teachers have the inherent skills to bring out the best in every student. Many students will have experienced trauma, and not just minoritised students.

Many of us, as well as our students, will have experienced adversity: situations and events that have caused pain, hurt, anguish and struggle. These situations are not limited to minoritised communities and it is very important to emphasise that.

The psychological impact of racism, often termed 'race-based trauma', is a growing area of study. This concept recognises the cumulative harm caused by experiences of racial discrimination, from overt acts to subtle microaggressions, leading to significant mental and emotional distress. Lived experiences like racist assaults, hate crimes or sexual violence can be deeply traumatic, and studies have shown that experiencing frequent microaggressions is also associated with increased anxiety, depression and post-traumatic stress symptoms. The historical legacy of racism, including slavery, segregation and systemic discrimination, has had a lasting effect on individuals and communities across generations. This can manifest in various ways, including mental health challenges, mistrust of authority and difficulty forming healthy relationships.

Students may face racist slurs on the walk to school. Black male students may experience racial profiling, such as being stopped and searched on public transport. Moments of social tension, like the riots in England during summer 2024, can create significant anxiety for Muslim, Black and South Asian students returning to school.

Religious identity is often marginalised, with students unable to access prayer spaces, compromising their sense of safety and belonging. Disabled students face constant physical barriers – limited wheelchair access in classrooms, corridors and physical education spaces – causing stress for both students and their parents. The persistent experiences of navigating a prejudiced society, encountering discrimination, racism and microaggressions, contribute to chronic stress and potential mental health challenges. These experiences extend beyond individual incidents, creating a cumulative impact on students' emotional and psychological wellbeing.

While this book focuses on creating equitable and safe environments, particularly for minorities and hidden voices in the classroom and schools, every student and adult may have experienced something that results in trauma. However, while teachers are experienced professionals, we do not all receive mental-health, trauma-informed training. Using the tools and strategies in this book, such as the classroom contract, wise interventions and having honest conversations with students, can help to support the wellbeing of our students too. Your school will have a safeguarding lead and perhaps an onsite counsellor or staff able to support students and provide you with advice and guidance on how to support students in your classroom too. Some brilliant resources about trauma-informed teaching and practices are included in the reference list at the end of this book.

You must also check in with yourself and take care of your own wellbeing. If you are feeling overwhelmed or struggling, seek advice from your trusted colleagues and charities such as Mind, which also offers brilliant support for adults.

Trauma leaves a lasting impact on an individual, affecting their wellbeing, physical and mental health. It can lead to a range of reactions in different situations which may 'trigger' their memory. Trauma and belonging are not isolated and cannot be addressed in silos. Creating a psychologically safe classroom is crucial for supporting students who may have experienced trauma, and is the subject of our next chapter.

5 Creating Psychological Safety

Picture this: a student hovers at your desk after class, clearly wanting to ask something but hesitating. Another keeps their hand half-raised during discussions, never quite committing to full participation. These moments – these small signs of uncertainty – tell us something crucial about our classroom environment.

This is where **psychological safety** comes in. According to Professor Amy Edmondson,[9] a leading expert on workplace dynamics, psychological safety exists when people feel able to ask questions, make mistakes and express their views, without fear of judgment or negative consequences. In the classroom, this means creating an environment where students feel secure enough to share their lived experiences and explore new knowledge, without worrying about feeling vulnerable or exposed.

Creating psychologically safe classrooms isn't just good practice – it's essential for building a culture where every student can truly belong. Think about it: students spend more waking hours at school than almost anywhere else. Our classrooms should feel like spaces where they can breathe easily, take intellectual risks and be authentically themselves. Students are effectively in secondary and further education for more than five years, and adolescent years are critical development years, too: developing a sense of belonging at school can have a positive impact on adolescent health, particularly emotional and mental health and wellbeing.[10]

Classroom culture

We need to focus on classroom culture to create classrooms where students feel psychologically safe from the outset. 'Culture' can feel like a vague and abstract word, but when thinking about the classroom, the framework on the following pages can help to make it a little more tangible.

Establishing routines

How do you begin each lesson? A consistent and welcoming routine can set the tone for the entire class. How do you greet students when they enter the classroom

---

[9] https://hbr.org/2023/02/what-is-psychological-safety
[10] https://pmc.ncbi.nlm.nih.gov/articles/PMC9600165

and how do they greet you? Do students know what is expected of them when they enter your classroom? For example, is it a silent entry with students standing behind their chairs waiting to be seated? Is it, 'Come in, take a seat, get your resources out and complete the activity on the board?' Or is it, 'Come in, take a seat, and have a quick chat with the person sitting next to you about how they're doing for a couple of minutes?' It can help to reflect on how this first entry can make students (and you) feel about the atmosphere for the next 60 minutes.

Creating an inclusive seating plan

Creating an inclusive seating plan needs to happen before your students step into the classroom. Spend some time gathering information about their needs and preferences – check through SEND documentation, have quiet chats with students about what works for them, and touch base with their previous teachers about successful strategies. Watch carefully during those first few lessons too – they'll tell you a lot about how your class works together.

Start with physical needs. Make sure students who have visual or hearing impairments can see and hear clearly. Think about space for mobility equipment, and consider who might need quick access to the door for breaks. Getting these basics right sets up your classroom for everyone to access the learning.

Next, think about learning needs. Some students will do better when they're positioned where you can easily check in with them, while others might thrive working alongside peers who complement their learning style. Keep in mind potential distractions – what works well for one student might be challenging for another.

The social side of seating plans needs careful thought. While it might be tempting to split up friends or separate the chattier students, sometimes friendship groups can actually support learning. Ask yourself:

- How can you balance social connections with focused learning?
- Which students might help to build each other's confidence?
- Where will quieter or anxious students feel most comfortable joining in?

Keep in mind that seating plans aren't permanent. Keep an eye on how well it's working, check in with your students now and then, and be ready to make changes as your class dynamics develop throughout the year. A truly inclusive seating plan grows and adapts with your class. To make this manageable alongside everything else, try these time-saving approaches:

- Keep a simple digital template of your classroom layout that you can quickly update.

- Use your school's management system to flag key information about student needs – many systems let you add notes directly to the seating plan.
- Take quick photos of arrangements that work well, so you can replicate them easily.
- Most importantly, build in five minutes at the end of each week to jot down any observations about how the seating is working – this saves you having to rely on memory when it's time to make changes.

You might also find it helpful to coordinate with colleagues who teach the same groups. Share what works (and what doesn't) in your regular department meetings or via your usual communication channels. This kind of collaboration can save everyone time and help build consistency across subjects.

Remember, you don't need to achieve the perfect seating plan immediately. Start with addressing essential needs, then adjust gradually as you get to know your class better. This approach is often more effective than trying to get everything right from day one.

Clearly defined expectations

Ensure students understand what is expected of them in terms of behaviour, participation, and completing tasks. Belonging does not need to mean an absence of expectations and boundaries. Not every student may appreciate the expectations and boundaries. However, over time, they will understand the necessity of these expectations and boundaries in establishing a culture of belonging, mutual respect and an impactful learning environment.

It can help you and students to have a clear and transparent understanding of what is expected at the beginning of every lesson, when you ask a question, or when group work, individual work or paired work is completed. Can students select their pairings and groups to work in? Is the latter a decision you can make collectively with your class?

At the beginning of the school year, new term, or even a new week, it helps to spend some time reminding the class and yourself of the expectations and boundaries in your classroom so that students have a clear understanding of them. This will contribute to a culture of belonging and psychological safety in the classroom.

Fostering a sense of belonging

What do students see when they enter your classroom? What posters do you have on display? What quotations (if any), people and examples of work do you have on display? Is the classroom contract on display? Just like in a home, décor can make a positive difference to the way a student feels in your classroom. Teachers take a lot of pride in displays and rightly so: a classroom environment can be an extension of you (particularly if you are lucky to be based in one classroom for all or most of your lessons!).

Ask students how the displays and classroom décor make them feel and think. What would they like to see? How can they contribute to your displays? The latter can also lead to students respecting displays and the classroom settings if they feel involved in them too. None of this need be time-consuming and it might be that not every student wishes to contribute – and that is OK. Creating a culture of belonging in displays and a classroom setting can be a collaborative approach between you, fellow teachers and a range of students with the aim of ensuring it is inclusive for every student, so that they feel that they belong.

Creating a safe space for expression

How can students let you know if they feel uncomfortable? Or, more importantly, do students know they can speak to you if something bothers them? The answer, I'm sure, is always a yes, but how do students know this? Are there displays encouraging this? Is this a message you share regularly? All of these questions are important to consider to foster safe spaces for expression in your classroom.

ADDRESSING INAPPROPRIATE COMMENTS

Despite our best efforts, even the most well-intentioned classroom rules can't prevent every awkward, cringeworthy, or downright hurtful comment that might slip out during a lesson. As teachers, we've all been there – that moment when a student says something that makes you want to run away. But here's the thing: these uncomfortable moments are actually golden opportunities for learning. This section dives into how we can turn those challenging interactions into powerful teachable moments that not only redirect inappropriate comments but also help students to develop empathy, self-awareness and a deeper understanding of respectful communication.

Create a clear protocol for addressing inappropriate or harmful comments. Discuss this with students at the beginning of the year and reinforce it throughout the term. If a student makes an inappropriate or ignorant comment about race, gender, religion, sexual orientation and more, how is this addressed in your classroom?

First, it needs to be addressed in front of the entire class to let all of the students know that inappropriate and ignorant comments are not acceptable. It is important that you make this visible, to make it clear to all students that their peers will be held accountable for their actions.

Depending on the nature of the comments, they could be addressed in a conversation after the lesson, when you have time to talk to the student. It is important to explain to the student how their comments may impact others, by making them feel excluded, unhappy or sad. Reinforce that the classroom is a learning environment and the culture you have all agreed to is a nurturing one where everyone feels comfortable and safe, but also one where you are able to address discomfort and ignorance, so that you can all continue to learn and build a culture of inclusion and belonging.

You are the best person to guide this conversation with the student. However, remember that you don't have to do it alone. Feel free to consult with a colleague, your head of department or the inclusion lead, especially if you're unsure how to address the specific comments made. Every classroom is different, and seeking support can be so valuable. If the comments are in breach of the school's behaviour and discrimination policy, or you suspect that they are, then you can follow the policy guidance.

You might be wondering, *'What if I miss these inappropriate comments?'* or *'What if I'm not aware they're harmful?'* The truth is, even if you don't catch something in the moment, you'll likely find out soon enough. Another student might report it, or you'll hear about it from a colleague who's noticed similar behaviour in a different class. You can still address these issues effectively, even after the fact. Remember to be kind to yourself – we're all learning, and these experiences are often new to teachers too.

Keep in mind that in classrooms, there's a real difference between students making comments that are just a bit off base and those that are genuinely hateful. While you'll need to deal with any discriminatory comments through proper disciplinary channels, those awkward but well-meaning comments often create a ripple effect – you'll spot it when students start speaking up to challenge them, or when the room's body language shifts from relaxed to tense. Watch for those crossed arms and exchanged glances!

Intersectionality and psychological safety

As teachers, we see **intersectionality** play out in our classrooms every day, even if we don't always name it. When we understand that each student's experiences are shaped by multiple overlapping aspects of their identity – their race, gender, family background, learning style and more – we can better support their unique needs. For instance, a Muslim girl who's also dyslexic might face different challenges from her peers who share just one of these characteristics. Understanding these intersections helps us to create more nuanced, effective support strategies.

'Lived experience' is about the things you learn from your own life. It's not just about what you see, but also how you feel and think about your experiences. For example, someone who has experienced homelessness can share valuable insights that can help others to understand and address this issue.

Intersectionality and individual lived experiences need to be at the centre of psychologically safe classrooms. In essence, the term 'intersectionality', coined by Professor Kimberlé Crenshaw, means there are different elements and parts to our identities, and our lived experiences are made up of various forms of inequality, be that race, religion, gender, age, disability and socioeconomic circumstances. Creating a truly inclusive classroom means helping students to see beyond their own immediate experiences. It's about building empathy through genuine connection – recognising that while we might not fully understand every aspect of someone else's identity, we can find common ground through shared human experiences. When students learn to listen and appreciate the diverse stories around them, they start to develop a deeper sense of understanding.

This isn't about forcing uncomfortable conversations or putting students on the spot, but about creating gentle, organic opportunities for students to recognise each other's humanity. Maybe it's through carefully designed group discussions, reflective writing or shared storytelling, where students can voluntarily share parts of their identity they feel comfortable exploring. The magic happens when students realise that beneath surface differences, there are universal experiences of hope, challenge, joy and belonging that connect us all.

While this book focuses on creating a sense of belonging for all students and communities in the classroom, it is also important to recognise that belonging and feeling included in our classrooms may not be as easy or straightforward for minoritised communities. For example, if a student is fasting during Ramadan, they may experience lessons and learning differently during that month. If a dyslexic student requires adapted resources and they are new to your class, they may not feel comfortable raising their hand and asking. If a non-binary student overhears another student asking, 'Why should I share my pronouns?', it may make them feel uncomfortable or exasperated. 'Belonging bites' (see Chapter 6) are a helpful tool to support inclusive language and communication in the classroom. After George Floyd's murder, I heard the phrase 'all lives matter' repeatedly while working as a diversity and inclusion lead in schools, which caused anger and upset for Black and racially minoritised students.

These are just a few examples – there are so many instances where minoritised communities feel they intentionally need to work harder to fit in, adapt or conceal things about their identity to belong in school. If they aren't proactively addressed, these situations can lead to tension, disagreements and conflict in schools, between students and staff, all of which affect your culture of belonging.

In 2021, the *Guardian* reported that exclusion rates are five times higher in certain parts of England for Black Caribbean students, compared to other ethnic groups.[11] According to a 2021 report, 'Just Like Us', published by an LGBTQ+ charity for young people, LGBTQ+ young people still feel disproportionately unsafe in schools and 68 per cent of LGBTQ+ young people reported that their mental health suffered more over the pandemic compared to 49 per cent of non-LGBTQ+ young people.[12] The report also revealed that Black LGBTQ+ students, disabled LGBTQ+ students and LGBTQ+ students eligible for free school meals felt more lonely and isolated over the pandemic, in comparison with other LGBTQ+ young people. Research and reporting into intersectional belonging in the classroom is still scarce, however, these reports and statistics reveal that marginalised identities and under-resourced groups in schools are more likely to feel less psychologically safe in school.

We, as teachers and the wider school community, need to work harder and with the intention to ensure our schools and classrooms are for everyone, where everyone can be their authentic selves, engage in discourse that cherishes and acknowledges diverse lived experiences and ultimately, classrooms where all students feel safe, supported and connected. This may include:

- Inviting students to share things about their cultures and lived experiences during particular cultural days and culture weeks. These occasions mustn't be just for students to 'dress up' but are an opportunity to learn about one another. Religious and cultural holidays are an excellent opportunity for these learning experiences, particularly for Key Stage 3 students (it may be that Key Stage 4 and 5 students lead on these activities and events).
- Extracurricular clubs and events, such as a culture club, Pride group, religious societies, and diversity and anti-racism clubs, can help create opportunities for students to learn and understand different lived experiences and, most importantly, help to empower students to contribute to school and classroom cultures. They can share what can help and support belonging in classroom and at school.

Student-led clubs and activities, though extracurricular, provide valuable spaces for exploring identity and lived experiences. Like workplace staff networks, they offer important avenues for engagement. Getting students to lead these clubs – such as Pride Club, Islam Club and Culture Club – reduces teacher workload while maintaining necessary adult supervision for safeguarding.

---

[11] www.theguardian.com/education/2021/mar/24/exclusion-rates-black-caribbean-pupils-england
[12] www.justlikeus.org/wp-content/uploads/2021/11/Just-Like-Us-2021-report-Growing-Up-LGBT.pdf

While some students may be reluctant to join clubs with teacher supervision, clear explanation of safety requirements and consistent messaging about these being safe, trusting spaces can help. Attendance often grows organically as students see their peers participating. Building this sense of belonging takes time and conscious effort, but student allies can help to encourage wider participation.

Take an empathetic approach to understanding students' intersectional lived experiences. While this kind of sharing often works well in subjects like English, History, RE, PSHE, Philosophy, Psychology and Science, remember that not all students will want to participate – and that's fine. Creating space for students to share their experiences, particularly those from minoritised backgrounds, gives them voice in both the conversation and the solutions process, but it must remain an invitation, not a requirement.

To encourage sharing:

- Explain intersectionality (see page 47) and how listening to others' experiences helps to build mutual understanding among peers.
- Acknowledge that sharing aspects of identity can feel both exciting and vulnerable – normalise these mixed feelings for students.
- Use curriculum-relevant examples, such as:
    - When reading *An Inspector Calls*, explore how different characters might react to Eva's dismissal based on their own experiences of class and privilege. Compare responses from her working-class friends versus middle-class characters who haven't experienced employment insecurity. While students might challenge this as a generalisation, it opens valuable discussions about how lived experiences shape perspectives.
    - In PE, discuss gender disparities in professional sports, including pay gaps and audience attendance, even after recent successes like the Women's World Cup. Encourage students to reflect on their own experiences – what sports were they encouraged to play? How did this differ between siblings? What role did sports play in their family life? When approached naturally within the lesson's flow and with genuine curiosity, these discussions often yield candid, insightful perspectives that enrich everyone's understanding.

Psychological safety isn't just for the marginalised…

Psychological safety means creating an environment where pupils are trusted and feel safe. They can be honest with teachers and classmates, can speak up when they need to, and have the freedom and security to try new things or make mistakes. It's about people being able to be themselves in order to perform at their best without any risk to their mental wellbeing.

Psychological safety isn't just a DEIJB initiative. While dedicated spaces like Pride Club, religious or social justice groups and lunchtime rooms for neurodivergent students serve important purposes, their existence can raise complex questions about belonging and inclusion in our schools.

The concept of 'safe spaces' is often misunderstood. Some view them as exclusively for minoritised students, suggesting that mainstream spaces aren't adequately inclusive. This perception can be problematic for several reasons. First, it may imply that certain students need special accommodation while others don't. Second, it can reinforce the narrative that schools are inherently unsafe for marginalised young people – a concern that carries some weight when we look at disparities in school exclusions, SEND support, and experiences of care leavers, GTRSB students (see page 4), and LGBTQ+ young people.

While dedicated spaces play a vital role in supporting specific communities, we must ensure they don't inadvertently segregate or stigmatise. The goal isn't to create separate safe spaces, but to make every school space psychologically safe for all students. This means considering how different aspects of identity intersect and influence students' experiences, while ensuring all students – including allies – feel welcome in both dedicated and mainstream spaces.

Psychological safety benefits all students, not just those from minoritised backgrounds. When students find themselves in what Amy Edmondson calls the 'Learning Zone', they experience an optimal balance between challenge and capability. This state of psychological safety enables everyone to engage fully in learning and take intellectual risks.

To create this environment, you can:

- engage all students in defining what makes a space psychologically safe, exploring when and why such safety becomes especially crucial
- gather input from both students and staff about what creates classroom safety for everyone, emphasising that you welcome perspectives from all identities and lived experiences
- explore with your class how allies can actively support in maintaining these safe spaces.

These discussions serve multiple purposes: they centre student voice, inform your classroom contract, and contribute to the broader school vision. By taking this collaborative approach, psychological safety becomes woven into the fabric of daily classroom life rather than existing as a separate initiative.

TIP

Here's some example phrasing I've found useful to build a safe classroom environment:

'I really want you to feel at ease in our classroom.'

'What can I do to make sure you feel comfortable and safe here?'

'Please let me know if there's anything I can do to help.'

...but marginalised communities are the least likely to feel safe

However, particularly with the rise of social media, the COVID-19 pandemic and in a post-Black Lives Matter era, the uncomfortable reality is that there are groups of students, particularly from marginalised communities, for whom the classroom is not particularly safe.

In many classrooms, students may not feel truly comfortable taking risks or expressing themselves freely, even when teachers strive to create a supportive environment. This can stem from several factors, such as an excessive focus on grades, unconscious biases in teacher interactions, fear of peer judgment, high-pressure assessments, or a lack of opportunities for open exploration. These factors can create an environment where students prioritise avoiding mistakes over genuine learning, hindering their intellectual growth and overall wellbeing.

One student who identified with the LGBTQ+ community explained that, during independent work, when sitting in front of a couple of students making remarks about them, they felt 'trapped' and 'ashamed' of telling the teacher. When I asked them if they felt safe, their response was 'yes, in general', but that moments like this are hard to navigate 'on your own'. When I listened to this I was sad but unsurprised, too.

CASE STUDY

Let's just agree to disagree

Ben, 14, recalls walking into an English lesson with a variety of motivational and thought-provoking quotes displayed around the room. As an aside, he told his teacher he would quite like to see a quote by Ronald Raegan up on the wall as he was really interested in Raegan at the time. The teacher replied, 'No, I won't have a quote by Raegan up on the wall.' Although the teacher and Ben expressed their thoughts, the conversation ended there. Ben says to create psychologically safe classrooms, 'Ask me why I disagree, or why I think what I do, as opposed to expecting me or other students to just agree with you.'

For several students, being able to discuss opposing viewpoints and being OK with disagreeing with each other came up as a core part of a psychologically safe classroom, which teachers can facilitate. 'I'm not saying you need to have Neo-Nazis running around, but classrooms are a place to have interesting debates and discussions,' Edward, 17, said. It's great having discussions with people who think the same, but this just creates another 'dangerous echo chamber', even within the classroom, 'plus, we don't learn very much'.

According to Ben, simple prompts from teachers such as, 'It's OK to have different viewpoints' or, 'it's OK to disagree and not hate each other!' can really help to open up a class debate and ensure different people are seen and heard – a core element of belonging in schools. In Maths and Science, he said it's not that they have difficult or sensitive conversations as they would in subjects like History and English, but the teacher has a way of making all students feel safe: 'There is no immense pressure. We do the work; it feels very natural and we have open discussions. We question each other's answers. I don't feel worried in Maths.'

This teacher has established a collaborative learning environment, where there is a trusting relationship between the teacher and their students, clear expectations and boundaries. All of this can be achieved by creating class contracts, which can support brave and uncomfortable conversations in the classroom (see page 67 in Chapter 6).

Misogynistic banter and sexist jokes are often at the centre of masculine expression in classrooms, particularly with the rise of social media trends, viral postings and the dreaded comments sections. It usually occurs during group work, is whispered, and is communicated when students are waiting outside a classroom or when they know a teacher cannot hear them. Students may not report it because, like with many things in the classroom, they respond in the heat of the moment and before we know it, a teacher is getting on with the main subject of the lesson. While teachers manage the bulk of behaviour in lessons, no teacher can hear and see every single thing said and done in a classroom, or outside.

Student responses to anxiety

This can leave students feeling worried, anxious and vulnerable; feelings that can manifest in different ways:

- Students may be eager to please their teachers by trying to answer a range of questions, taking the lead in group activities and sometimes doing extra work for validation.

- Students may seem quiet, 'shy', unwilling to volunteer and would rather work quietly and independently.
- Students may attempt to consistently talk to their peers, entertain in lessons, which is often seen as disruptive behaviour.
- Students may disengage from certain tasks or present inconsistent behaviour and attitudes depending on the class task or topic.

Of course, all, some or none of the above may apply and they are not limited to marginalised groups of students; this makes a teacher's job all the more complex and all the more valuable too.

Psychological safety outside the classroom

I recently had an eye-opening conversation with a group of cis male secondary school students that really made me think. Do you know where they told me they felt least safe? Not in lessons, but in those in-between spaces – queuing for lunch, hanging out in the playground, even just waiting outside classrooms. It hit me right in the heart, honestly. Here we are, teaching these wonderful young people who, despite their teenage bravado, still need us around just to feel secure.

This kind of insight really shows why we need to think bigger than just our individual classrooms. In my experience, the magic happens when everyone in the school community gets involved. Those lunchtime supervisors, counsellors, teaching assistants? They're absolute gold. Too often we forget to include them in conversations about belonging and safety, but they see our students in completely different contexts from us. Their insights can be game-changing.

I've found that building a web of support works wonders. It starts with us modelling the kind of respectful, inclusive behaviour we want to see, but it grows when we actively encourage students to look out for each other. Those peer relationships can be incredibly powerful – both academically and socially. Being visible makes a huge difference too. If your timetable allows (and I know that's a big 'if'!), try to pop up in unexpected places – the corridors, the canteen, those spaces where students have told us they feel less secure. It's not about policing; it's about presence.

TIP

Teach students about the 90-second rule for managing emotions. It takes just about that long for an emotional response to physically process through your body.[13] Teaching students to count down during tense moments gives them a concrete tool for handling conflict.

Lastly, make sure students know exactly how to report concerns when they need to. I'm a big fan of putting this information everywhere, especially in those spaces where students have said they feel vulnerable. In my experience, when we weave all these approaches together, that's when we really start to see every student feeling secure throughout their entire school day. The key is remembering that while we're experts in our subjects, we're also essentially caretakers of these young people's sense of safety and belonging. It's a big responsibility, but when we work together – staff, students, and school community – it's amazing what we can achieve.

[13]www.psychologytoday.com/gb/blog/the-right-mindset/202004/the-90-second-rule-builds-self-control

6 Creating a 'Safe Classroom'

Given that schools are community-driven environments where most students spend several years with a similar group of peers, navigating the same hallways, becoming familiar with a consistent set of teachers, and generally adhering to established routines, they are ideal settings for fostering psychological safety.

The challenge of creating psychological safety

Psychological safety is perhaps the simplest and most difficult feeling to achieve in the classroom. I say this because classrooms can be vulnerable spaces and building trust with teenagers is a sensitive and mindful process.

Creating a psychologically safe classroom is a complex and ongoing process. While psychological safety is relatively straightforward, achieving it in practice can be challenging.

The goal is clear: to create an environment where students feel comfortable, respected, and free to learn without fear of judgment or ridicule, and concepts like respect, empathy and inclusivity are generally understood and accepted.

However, there are so many factors which can make implementing these principles in a real-world classroom setting quite complex. Each student has unique needs and experiences. Creating a safe space that addresses the diverse needs of all students requires careful consideration and ongoing adaptation. Building strong, trusting relationships with students takes time and effort. Dealing with disruptive or inappropriate behaviour requires sensitivity, consistency and a focus on restorative practices, and fostering open and respectful dialogue while addressing sensitive or controversial topics requires careful guidance and facilitation. Therefore, while the goal of creating a psychologically safe classroom is clear, achieving it in practice requires ongoing effort, reflection, and a commitment to continuous improvement.

Mitigating the 'interpersonal risks' to create psychologically safe classrooms

As mentioned above, Professor Edmondson's research about psychological safety can also be applied to the classroom. In secondary school classrooms, the interpersonal risks that can affect psychological safety are:

- not knowing your peers
- being aware of your minoritised identity, whether that is race, religion, culture, gender, disability or neurodiversity
- the impression teachers or fellow students may have of an individual's identity, race, religion, disability, neurodiversity, sex or gender
- 'coming from' different primary school settings, home school settings and international settings
- not knowing where to sit in a classroom, or having someone to sit next to
- the perception and judgement of peers and teachers
- the fear of not 'fitting in'
- the fear of not belonging to the 'popular group' or having a recognisable group of friends in every lesson
- not using or being less active on social media
- fear of expressing a different opinion or thought *because* it is just that: different from the mainstream or dominant narrative.

ACTIVITY

What would you add to the list above?

When thinking about your students in different year groups and different times of the year (particularly around festivals, cultural and religious holidays), what other factors would you add to the list above which impact psychological safety in the classroom?

Looking at your list, what things do you do on a daily, weekly or termly basis that work towards developing psychological safety?

- Do you have a calendar of holidays on display in your classroom?
- Do you check in with students who may be impacted by certain holidays and events across the year, such as Hanukkah, Ramadan, Passover, Diwali and more?
- Do you offer opportunities in form time, PSHE, a club or in your lesson where students can talk about current events that may have an impact on them, or that they would simply like to talk about with you?
- Do you have various options for assessment that are adapted to different student needs? Some students, particularly at Key Stage 3, may perform better

with verbal evaluations compared to written assessments, or they may prefer short answer questions over long-form prose. While certain exam requirements at GCSE and A levels are unavoidable and beyond a teacher's control, we can address feedback from students if they find a long-form essay overwhelming. To overcome this, we can offer different assessment options. At Key Stage 3, we can implement flexible and inclusive assessment styles to help build student confidence. This approach will foster psychological safety and, in the long run, encourage students to explore various assessment methods

- Do students have inclusion passports, in which they can share their individual needs with you as their teacher, and with fellow students (during group work, for example)?

Keep this list handy to share with colleagues, particularly colleagues new to your school and community, so you can work together to create consistent, psychologically safe classrooms.

In secondary school, students move from class to class, not always with the same group of students or the same teacher. For students who have just come from primary school, the transition is overwhelming and it can take the entire first year of secondary school for things to settle. Equally, moving from term to term, year to year, with ongoing changes from class to friendship groups can all impact students' sense of psychological safety. Students may not feel represented in their classes, or by their teachers.

One student in Key Stage 3, Aran, told me that, as much as he wanted to tell a teacher when another was laughing at him, he didn't want to be a 'snitch' either. We must be explicit about our culture of belonging, continually emphasising the class contract and that the classroom is a safe space for every student. Referring back to the school values, and holding students accountable for their actions, can reassure minoritised students that they are safe, that we are allies, and that they can also advocate for themselves in your classroom.

What makes a classroom 'safe'?

We've talked about what psychological safety means in theory, but what does it actually look like in practice? How do we know when we've created it successfully? I posed this question to Dan, an Assistant Headteacher and Head of Sixth Form, who regularly observes dozens of different classrooms.

'You can feel it the moment you walk through the door,' he explains. 'In a psychologically safe classroom, there's a warmth to the atmosphere. Students are engaged, often smiling. When someone makes a mistake or offers an unusual perspective, their classmates respond with interest rather than judgment. Any negativity gets gently but firmly challenged, not by the teacher alone, but by the students themselves.'

This description might sound idealistic, but it's achievable. The key lies in understanding that psychological safety isn't something we create once and tick off our list – it's something we actively maintain through hundreds of small interactions every day.

When speaking to a group of students a while ago, they told me about an activity they'd done in PSHE where they had to list 'unsafe things' that may be said to minoritised communities. They found this very uncomfortable and, of course, it was not a positive experience for the LGBTQ+ students and other minoritised students in the classroom.

Instead, ask students what makes a classroom and school safe for them. They can refer to one another too, but in the first instance, ask students to reflect on their own experiences, thoughts and feelings about safety so they can articulate on sticky notes what a safe classroom looks like. What would they like to see and hear? This can be completed using sticky notes, which you can display in the classroom.

This can gently develop into a more general discussion about what they don't want to see and hear. This does not need to be articulating specific comments, but you may find they say that every student should feel welcome and should not experience discrimination or hurtful language and actions.

Seen, heard and represented

I asked Frances Akinde, education consultant and ex-headteacher specialising in SEND, how to create a culture of inclusion and belonging for SEND and neurodivergent students in our classrooms.

> ***'SEND and neurodiverse secondary school students may feel isolated in classrooms where they are a minority. Transitioning from primary to secondary can often be difficult for students and their parents. How can teachers create environments that don't isolate or make SEND students uncomfortable?'***
>
> *'Imagine being in a classroom where you feel like the odd one out. That's often the reality for SEND and neurodiverse students. The jump from primary to secondary school can be a rollercoaster for the students and their parents, too. Teachers can make a world of difference by creating a safe and inclusive environment. Think about personalised learning plans catering to each student's unique needs, or having designated safe spaces where they can take some time to breathe if things get too overwhelming. Pairing them with an understanding buddy through pupil support programmes can also help them feel*

more connected. But fundamentally, first and foremost, teacher training should be where educators are equipped with the right tools and strategies.'

'How can teachers and schools create classrooms that are safe spaces for SEND/ neurodiverse students from the moment a parent and student starts interacting with the school?'

'Students should feel welcomed and supported when they step into a school. Schools can achieve this by having clear, inclusive policies and engaging with parents and students early on. Visual supports like schedules and signs can help students navigate the new environment more quickly. Sensory-friendly spaces with reduced sensory input can be a haven for those who need it. It's all about the school making every student feel like they belong from the beginning.'

'Student to student: how can teachers educate students without the lived experiences or even awareness of SEND to be allies and respectful of one another?'

'It's crucial to educate all students about neurodiversity and SEND to foster a culture of respect and understanding. Peer mentorship programmes can encourage 'neurotypical' students to support their neurodiverse classmates. Open discussions about diversity and inclusion can also help address any stigmas head on. It's about creating a community where everyone feels valued and understood.'

Get the basics right

I asked LGBTQ+ education consultant and founder of QueerEd consultancy David Church to share his expertise on creating a culture of belonging for LGBTQ+ students. While you can use several points in this book to create and nurture safety and belonging for the LGBTQ+ community, it is really important to amplify the voices of marginalised communities, particularly communities that are often made vulnerable in the media and in classrooms.

David advises that optics matter, and getting the basics right is crucial, so that students can see representation of LGBTQ+ individuals (for example, in lesson activities, on displays, in careers and PSHE sessions, and as guest speakers) across their school environment. This may be:

- lanyards that have the LGBTQ+ colours and flag
- posters of LGBTQ+ role models with different lived experiences and intersectional identities
- diverse and representative role models; maybe house names, curriculum topics, external speakers and more which are visible to students

- an extracurricular club for LGBTQ+ students to come together to build a community and network, which can be very helpful for students who feel vulnerable or just want to meet students who are a part of their community.

  Note that these groups may require dedicated staff support or student mentors. Ensure these groups are accessible to all students who wish to participate. Emphasise confidentiality and create a safe and supportive environment within these groups.

When considering guest speakers, remember that someone who identifies as LGBTQ+ doesn't have to speak only about LGBTQ+ topics. For example, you might invite a financial advisor to talk about adolescent finances, and they could also be part of the LGBTQ+ community. In your advocacy, let others know that you welcome guests who want to share their experiences and perspectives. This approach can help break down barriers and make students feel recognised and included in various settings, showing them they can belong not just in your classroom, but in many different spaces, just like the diverse role models you invite.

Mispronouncing names: a form of microaggression

Let me share something that transformed my own teaching practice: understanding the power of names. We might think mispronouncing a student's name is a minor issue – an honest mistake that happens once or twice. But research tells us something different. The way we handle students' names can profoundly affect how they see themselves and their place in our classroom.

There's even a term for this – the '**hedonic marking hypothesis**' – which explains why we tend to favour things (including names) that feel easy and familiar. This even happens when you control for things like how long the name is or how unusual it sounds. It shows that subtle factors, like how easy a name is to say, can unconsciously influence our opinions and decisions. Sometimes this manifests as giving anglicised nicknames or changing people's names entirely, but the practice of changing names has a deeply troubling history, and is often associated with oppression and the suppression of cultural identity (e.g. indigenous communities and slavery in the US).

But here's the thing: no name is inherently difficult. When we find a name challenging to pronounce, that's usually about our own linguistic background, not about the name itself. A name that's common in one culture may sound unfamiliar or difficult to pronounce to someone from a different cultural background.

I learned this lesson early in my teaching career when a group of students told me that I'd been pronouncing another student's name incorrectly for almost a year (a brilliant example of allyship)! The student hadn't wanted to correct me in front of others, but the mispronunciation was bothering her, even though she kept saying, 'It's fine.' That conversation was candid and appreciated by me – and I corrected my mistake.

It's crucial to help staff and students to recognise that lack of familiarity with a name often reflects a lack of exposure to a language or culture, rather than any inherent flaw in the name itself.

Students have noticed that, when sharing pronouns or if a name is mispronounced, there can be awkward glances or subtle negative movements in body language across the classroom from other students, felt by minoritised students. They do not often feel comfortable addressing them, because they are so swift. Confronting this in a classroom setting with their peers can be difficult. These incidents have a real impact on students' self-confidence, social and emotional wellbeing, and even academic performance. Our names are one of the most basic parts of our identity. Of course, this isn't easy to control and, in some ways, is to be expected if students are not accustomed to discussing diversity or being in a diverse classroom environment.

You might find the following ideas helpful:

- As students walk into the classroom for the first time, greet them and ask them what their names are. It is a straightforward strategy that can help with pronunciation in a one-to-one exchange, avoiding silence and awkward exchanges later on. Teachers often express concern about mispronouncing names; this often happens when we are learning student names for the very first time when calling out a register in a public space (the first lesson). Students will often be OK with how you pronounce their name (even if it is not how they want you to pronounce it) because they have become accustomed to people mispronouncing it. If they recognise it is them that you are talking to, they will say yes and respond. However, it is empowering for a young person to be asked, 'How do I pronounce your name? I will ensure I get it right, but please correct me if I mispronounce it in class.' It creates a subtle yet powerful feeling of trust between a student and teacher, one where a student is seen.
- A one-to-one exchange may seem time-consuming; however, it is important to remember that some names you will be able to say very easily and some you may just need to jot down the phonetic spelling (there is nothing wrong with this – it is how many of us teach children how to read, of course!). Putting in this extra time at the beginning of the first couple of lessons will help to develop a personable relationship with students from the beginning of the school year.

> **TIP**
>
> Simple statements like the one below can set an inclusive tone and create an environment which shows students they belong and are seen in your classroom:
>
> *'My name is pronounced "Za – haaa – ra". Please share the phonetic pronunciation of your name too as I would like to make sure I say your name how you would like me to.'*

- Be an active ally: if you witness someone mispronouncing another person's name, gently and respectfully correct them.
- Respect individual choices: ultimately, the decision to change one's name is a personal one. Respect an individual's choice to use the name they prefer, regardless of whether it's their given name, a chosen name or a nickname.
- Instead of focusing on 'easy' or 'difficult' names, we should acknowledge that names are inherently loaded with social and cultural meaning. Every name carries a history, evokes certain associations, and signals social and cultural identities, for example, gender, social class, ethnicity and nationality or cultural trends. These social cues inevitably influence how people perceive and interact with individuals. Recognising this inherent social and cultural significance of names is crucial for understanding their impact on our perceptions and judgments.

Students have commented that the simple act of pronouncing their names correctly or asking about their pronouns subtly begins the process of developing an inclusive classroom. Of course, this is common practice in many schools.

Sharing pronouns

Pronouns are words used to identify individuals beyond their name, including traditional pronouns like I, you, she, her, they, them, and inclusive pronouns like ze, hir, hirs.[14] These are particularly important for non-binary individuals who may not identify with binary gender terms.

---

[14]These are examples of **neopronouns** – alternative pronouns that some people use instead of she/he/they. Here's how they work:

Ze (pronounced 'zee') is used in place of she/he/they as a subject pronoun. For example: 'Ze went to the store.'

Hir (pronounced like 'here') is used as both an object pronoun (like him/her/them) and a possessive adjective (like his/her/their). For example: 'I gave the book to hir' or 'That is hir book.'

Hirs (pronounced like 'heres') is used as a possessive pronoun (like his/hers/theirs). For example: 'The book is hirs.'

Being misgendered can be deeply hurtful, especially for trans and non-binary individuals. Respecting someone's pronouns is crucial in acknowledging their identity and creating an inclusive environment. It shows basic human respect and helps combat the stigma and discrimination these communities often face.

In educational settings, creating a safe space for pronoun-sharing is important. However, it should always be voluntary. As an educator, you can:

- model pronoun-sharing by introducing your own (if comfortable)
- create a welcoming classroom environment with inclusive language
- use gender-neutral terms like 'students' instead of 'guys' or 'girls'.

The goal is to create an environment where everyone feels respected and able to be their authentic self.[15]

TIP

A simple display poster in your classroom that reads: *'Please feel free share your pronouns with me and the class, if and when you feel comfortable to do so'* can make students feel comfortable and aware that yours is an inclusive classroom (as a teacher, you can share your pronouns too, but only if you feel comfortable doing so).

When addressing groups whose pronouns you haven't been told, use gender-neutral language. Instead of saying 'girls/guys/boys', opt for 'students'. Replace 'OK guys' with 'OK everyone' or 'Hello class'.

Adapting your language takes practice. Most of us are used to gendered terms, and it's normal to slip up. The key is to consciously correct yourself and keep learning. Each time you use inclusive language, it becomes more natural. Acknowledge mistakes, learn from them, and continue making an effort.

[15]For more information about pronouns please see: https://pronouns.org/what-and-why. There is so much useful information available online about the use of pronouns. The information is easy to read and time-efficient too, so a great way to learn about how to ally with the LGBTQ+ community.

TIP

We've moved on from using the term 'preferred gender pronoun' to simply 'pronouns'. This reflects a growing understanding that pronouns are not a preference, but form an integral aspect of an individual's identity. Using someone's correct pronoun is a fundamental act of respect and demonstrates a commitment to inclusivity and understanding.

Talking to parents – requesting 'belonging bites'

If your school is digitally enabled, students and parents may see an email from you before they see you 'IRL' (in real life – how we've all become accustomed to Zoom life!). 'Belonging bites' are something you could request and share via email. These are minor bitesize pieces of information that can have a macro impact on a student's sense of belonging in your classroom. As well as pronouns, you may request other information too, such as phonetic spelling of names, where in the classroom they may learn better (this may have an impact on seating plans) and other information that helps you to create a culture of belonging for them in your classroom. An act like this makes parents and students feel comfortable and safer entering your classroom. Some students may not want to share this information for various reasons, and that's OK. At this stage, you are 'setting the scene' and the expectation that your classroom will be a safe space for every student.

Communication and policies

It is important that parents, carers and relevant stakeholders are aware that your classroom and your school are safe spaces for LGBTQ+ learners, along with different minoritised communities too. This must be clarified from the outset, particularly during the transition from primary to secondary school. David advises not to underestimate the transition from primary school to secondary school, as several students will already be confident in their sexuality and/or gender identity. However, they may feel apprehensive about the transition if they do not see LGBTQ+ belonging and inclusion in their introduction to the school. It is important that you communicate information about belonging and inclusion from the moment parents and carers engage with your school. This is not just for minoritised communities; it informs the entire school community that inclusion, safety and belonging are at the heart of the school's culture and it is essential that this is respected by every member of the school community.

Drawing up a class contract/contracting

With the input of your class, draw up a 'class contract' with agreed mutual expectations, boundaries, dos and don'ts. As a teacher, this can also give you the space and time to address questions, concerns and even misconceptions students may have about the classroom. This is a great way to begin the new academic year and revisit at the beginning of each term. When students from all backgrounds feel that they have a voice, the culture of belonging can increase as they have invested in crafting their classroom culture.

For more engaged or able students you might use this phrase bank:

'Everyone is welcome in the classroom. This is a safe space where everyone will be seen, heard and respected. We all belong here.'

'We appreciate and recognise we all learn differently. Your teacher will ensure learning is catered to your different ways of learning. You can speak to them before or after lessons about ways to personalise learning for you.'

'We respect that we are a large class and everyone has different wants and needs. We will help each other to ensure everyone can learn together.'

'We understand everyone everyone has different lived experiences and viewpoints. We will use empathy and respect in our responses to each other, even if we disagree.'

'It is OK to disagree with one another. It is OK to agree. It is OK to change our minds, too. We don't focus on convincing others about our viewpoint when we have a discussion. Instead, we actively listen and learn from one another.'

'We will not interrupt or talk over one another as it is distracting and insensitive.'

'We will learn to laugh together and have fun when learning too.'

However, for younger students or those who benefit from more direct language, you can simplify these same principles. The key messages remain identical, but the language becomes more accessible and immediate:

'We're all in this together: Everyone belongs here, and we want to make sure everyone feels safe and respected.'

'We learn in different ways: We know that everyone learns differently, so your teacher will do their best to help you learn in the way that works best for you.'

'We respect each other's differences: we all have different ideas and opinions, and that's OK! We'll listen to each other respectfully, even when we disagree.'

'Let's work together: we'll help each other learn by being kind and supportive.'

> *'It's OK to make mistakes: learning involves trying new things, and that sometimes means making mistakes. It's OK to make mistakes – we learn from them!'*
>
> *'Learning should be enjoyable. Let's make the most of our time together and have some fun along the way.'*

Both contracts have the same aims for nurturing a culture of belonging and respect in your classroom. As we know, teenagers and adolescent students are ever-changing and teachers need to adapt the language they use with different key stages. The examples above can be used and adapted for Key Stages 3, 4 and 5 as you see fit for your classes.

Write the contract together and use the time to address any wider school rules too, like toilet breaks, homework policies and even seating plans. It can help to sense-check the contract to ensure compassion, respect and empathy are embedded throughout the document.

TIP

A useful prompt for getting the discussion going:

'Take five minutes to talk to the person next to you about how you want to feel, be seen, listened to, learn and engage in lessons.'

If you find there are differences between your class contract and wider school rules, or perhaps students have raised something about the school rules that can be addressed, you can discuss these concerns openly and honestly with your students. Explain the rationale behind the school rules and explore potential solutions together. Bring this up at a department meeting, with a Head of Year or member of senior leadership.

Encourage students to raise their concerns through appropriate channels, such as the student council, if you have one.

ACTIVITY

As well as with your students, it can help to draw up a similar contract with your department. This creates consistency across the department so students know what to expect no matter who their teacher is in that subject area. For example:

- Do all classes require a seating plan?
- How do you collectively address challenges and bias in the classroom?

- When can students speak to you outside of a lesson if they have a question or concern? Is this a specific lunchtime, breaktime or do you prefer students to make an appointment with you?
- How do you, as a department, want every student to *feel* in your classrooms? What do you collectively do to enable this feeling?

Some schools draw up whole-school contracts for conduct in classrooms. It is important to acknowledge that while there are similarities across all subject areas, each department will have distinct differences based on the subject, the dynamics and department culture. For example, Physical Education may share similarities with Design Technology, but there will be distinct differences with Modern Foreign Languages – and students may expect this too.

7 Having Brave Conversations

Teachers are best placed, and classrooms are the safest places, for these respectful, uncomfortable, brave and candid conversations.

The most valuable resource in any classroom is the teacher, and the most valuable asset a teacher has is their ability to listen and converse with young adults. Students can find a sense of belonging and safety in every classroom, and teachers can enable it. We don't need perfect teachers who always say and do the right thing; we need teachers that listen, and who feel confident and able to have brave conversations with all students. And, we need students who can listen too, who know they are safe, seen and can thrive in every classroom.

Challenges

In theory, allyship, creating a contract and teaching empathy sounds like a dream! However, going back to student responses, how do we deal with:

- *'What about if I don't want to share my pronouns? Why is this even "a thing"?'*
- *'What about if I'm not "mansplaining" and just trying to say what I think?'*
- *I get bullied for the way I look, and people are calling me racist when I'm not. What about the racism and bullying I'm getting?*
- *What about if I just don't care?*[16]

Things can very easily escalate in classrooms, especially during class discussions which, ironically, are when students are thoroughly engaged in learning and are a prime opportunity to navigate psychological trust and safety. In the moment, to manage behaviour and student voice, we may want to shut down conversations and discussions as they become uncomfortable. Instead, remind students about active listening and your contract:

- *'OK, let's pause. Let's listen to what the other person is thinking, feeling and saying.'*
- *'It's absolutely normal to feel angry, hurt, upset, annoyed (acknowledge how the students are feeling). We will discuss why we feel like this and explain our responses.'*

---

[16] See page 151 on 'whataboutisms' for further tips and advice on answering these types of questions.

- *'Let's take five minutes – everyone needs to pause and quietly think about their reasoning, opinions and justifications for their viewpoints. Everyone who would like to share an opinion will be given the opportunity to do that.'*

It really helps to ask students to pause and think about their reasoning. Psychological safety may be compromised if only the loudest voices are heard or if dominant viewpoints are heard. Teachers can facilitate and coordinate discussions so everyone has space and time to express their opinions with thoughtful reasoning. This can help curb **whataboutisms** and give students time to be with their thoughts before expressing themselves. It also encourages connection and understanding in the classroom – a key part of creating a culture of belonging for students.

Teachers want all students to feel safe but, when discussing the fear of making mistakes, one student mentioned that, while academic errors are accepted, there isn't the same freedom to make mistakes when it comes to discussing 'other things'. Students are not given the space to express their thoughts and views without the fear of being 'cancelled', 'called out' or demonised by their peers and people around them. One told me that everyone just expects them to 'know the right answer, when we don't'. They also said they feel there is an assumption that they would naturally talk to a teacher or their parents about what they see on social media or how they're feeling, which simply isn't the case. Using the questions and discussion starters throughout this chapter and Chapter 5 (on psychological safety), we can encourage students to share their thoughts candidly and respectfully, which may feel scary but they will also know they are in safe classroom environments that will help navigate these feelings too.

CASE STUDY

Just tell us the truth!

I once asked a student I taught many years ago, who was feeling disconnected from school and education, what they wanted from school. He responded, 'I just wanted them to tell us the truth. Sometimes, we're called into assemblies after an incident or something has happened. It's so unclear; no one understands what's going on, and we all leave looking at each other, thinking, 'Did that happen? What was that about? Just tell us straight.'

I remember rushing in to explain *why* a teacher or school may take this stance: they're trying to protect students, they don't have all the information to share, and it is inappropriate to share personal circumstances with a room full of students. I soon realised that wasn't what the students expected: they wanted some clarity and truth to maintain trust and respect for their schools. We can make this possible by addressing certain situations clearly and transparently.

Sanum, an Assistant Headteacher, has had some candid and sensitive conversations this year following the ongoing crisis in Gaza. However, her transparent approach with students has led to more trusting and positive relationships in school. Some students shared their frustrations with her about being unable to talk about what has been happening and feeling they were not being listened to. Sanum explained the positions teachers find themselves in: as well as fulfilling the 'day job', teachers and schools are having to intentionally keep up to date with the news and ensure their information is accurate and verified. Equally, while school is absolutely a place where students can have discussions and conversations about world events in a safe environment, it is a teacher's responsibility to ensure every student feels safe and included at school, reminding students that not everyone has access to the same information. Sanum facilitated lunchtime sessions that students and staff could attend to have conversations about Israel and Palestine.

The space was deliberately structured with mutual respect and an understanding of *what the space is for*: very similar to classroom **contracting** (see page 67). One student shared about their feelings and advocacy with Sanum. They shared that they appreciated the space and time created by the school to navigate such complex world events and now wanted to channel their energy into school and exams, with a long-term plan of working towards a career in which they could positively impact the world. Not only does this demonstrate a high level of emotional maturity and self-reflection, but also the positive impact truthful and trusting spaces can have on young people and their relationships with staff at school.

Facing your vulnerability

Dan, an Assistant Headteacher and Head of Sixth Form, has been leading his school's diversity and inclusion charter alongside the school's approach to difficult conversations and topics, such as the influence of Andrew Tate. Dan shared there have been some difficult conversations with students, in particular, following an assembly about his experience in South Africa:

> *'I did an assembly on race and spoke about my experience in South Africa, where we visited an area where the inhabitants referred to themselves as the "Cape Coloureds". I mentioned this as part of my talk and had a couple of [biracial] students with mixed ethnicity come up to me afterwards to say that I shouldn't have used that term... I obviously apologised, but knowing what words to use – for me, particularly around race as a white person – can be a real challenge. I have read Jeffrey Boakye's book* Race Unlisted *which essentially goes*

through all the different possible words explaining the negative connotations around them... It was a fascinating read but has left me even more confused about what I should be saying. Trying to be as educated about the topic as you can be is important but – as highlighted above – even if you are interested and try and learn, it can be tricky. Something we now are doing in our Year 8 and Year 9 PSHE lessons is having a pair of Sixth Formers in the class, too, so that they can support with discussions. They often have a better awareness of the latest terms being used and whether they are respectful or not.

[It is important to] be open and say that you're not an expert! Students are often very used to their teacher knowing the subject they're teaching really well, but there's a power in being open and honest and saying that we're all learning together about many of these aspects and how to navigate the best way towards creating a kind and caring world.'

Dan's candid reflection here mirrors what several teachers I speak to feel on a daily basis. Inclusion can be a vulnerable and unnerving space to navigate, particularly if we do not have shared experiences or an understanding of different lived experiences. As Dan rightly highlights, the truth (and power) is in remembering this is a journey of learning. As teachers in a school and classroom environment, we have a brilliant opportunity to support students with how to have respectful and challenging discussions and learn alongside them too.

With global events as they stand (or move) and the democratisation of knowledge through social media, we can apply these case studies to several situations. Many schools are finding it more and more challenging to address world events, whether it's Black Lives Matter, the Gaza crisis, Russia–Ukraine, student mental health, police brutality, and more. It is really hard, plus teaching and learning take up a significant amount of time (surprise, surprise!). But shutting down these conversations does not create a culture of belonging and trust. Instead, it increases frustration, uncertainty and disengagement too.

To support schools and teachers, it can help to respond transparently to these matters and follow up with a safe space where students can talk and ask questions. While you can't address everything centrally, classroom teachers will likely hear ripples when teaching. As a school or teacher, it can help to:

- Stop and acknowledge the discussion and concerns or questions raised; be transparent.
- Revisit the classroom contract and emphasise that your classroom is a safe and inclusive place for all students, so all discussions must be had respectfully. Disagreement is fine, so long as you're engaging in a discussion, not an argument.
- Listen if you can. Bear in mind there is no need to respond or provide a solution; just by listening, you create space for students to be seen and heard.

- Use the phrase banks on page 67 to create a compassionate environment where students can share their thoughts and be their authentic selves.

If you are unable to listen, or if your school has a different approach, signpost your students to a time or place where they can engage in these discussions. This may be during lunchtime, a debate club, a club set up for difficult discussion, or a time they can come and speak to you. It is important to create intentional spaces for these types of discussions. This is because, while we may want every student to be able to talk about anything and everything at any point of the school day, in reality, this is not always possible when you are time-bound by lessons, several other students, and operating in what is a high-stress environment! While creating intentional spaces also requires time and commitment, you will find that the conversations will be more meaningful and productive; they give you time and the headspace to prepare and be mindfully present for what can often be challenging conversations. Plus, setting aside time for topics and issues that clearly impact students also highlights that you respect the time and dedication required for discussions like these. By acknowledging the problem or concern, particularly for marginalised students, you are, in the first instance, creating space for students to feel seen, heard and listened to, therefore creating classrooms and schools which *belong to the students*.

Developing and nurturing a culture of transparency and discussion helps students to feel seen and heard. They may want to talk about an issue that the teacher has spotted and proactively addressed on social media, particularly if they feel passionate about it – and purpose and passion can also increase a student's sense of belonging and engagement in the classroom. While time is limited in the classroom, teachers have shared that it is possible to take 5–10 minutes to acknowledge and address an issue.

However, it is important to highlight here that it depends on the issue or topic. You may choose to use 5–10 minutes of the lesson to acknowledge the topic, for example, if something has been raised about a viral TikTok about Andrew Tate, a new celebrity diet trend, or an internet challenge that is causing conflict at breaktimes and lunchtimes, it may be that you:

- **Recognise** the issue in lesson: *'I understand that X is what many of us are talking and thinking about right now.'*
- **Acknowledge** a couple of the views about the issue: *'It seems some of us think this … and some of us disagree and think this … about it.'*
- **Respond** with how the issue will be addressed: *'Right now, we need to focus on the lesson, but if you go along to* [a debate club, student council, or suggest a break or lunchtime when students can speak to you about it], *we can have a conversation about it then.'*

- **Shift** the attention back to the lesson: *'For now, we've acknowledged the issue and that we need to talk about it. We've put in time to do that. Now, let's get back to the lesson.'*

Of course, there may still be a few whispers and students wanting to talk about it in the moment. This can feel unavoidable. However, over time, when students have experienced these conversations with you either in the lesson, or like above, at a dedicated time, they will begin to trust that you will give them that dedicated time and space. The more often we address **misinformation** and **disinformation**, and the challenging topics that are usually associated with these issues, the more likely we are to develop trust turning into positive and healthy relationships and conversation styles in our classrooms.

Act curious

Don't feel you need to conduct a full lesson or assembly on contentious or emotive topics. Instead, ask students what they know. Why do they like Andrew Tate (see Chapter 12)? What does he talk about? Engaging students in a critical conversation creates room for you, as the teacher, to question and critique their views and challenge pre-existing ideas without coming across as the adult attempting to 'lecture' or show them 'what's right'! Teachers can do this at form time, particularly if you know it is a topic that will come up throughout the school day. Form time, or the beginning of the day, is a great time to help frame the day, boundaries and expectations so that students (and you) can get on with the teaching day knowing that a critical topic or issue has been addressed. Equally, if something is raised at the beginning of the day that you find needs to be addressed later on, it gives you some time (if needed) to decide whether to address the topic the following day, at a lunchtime, or raise it with fellow teachers to be aware and mindful of. The latter via email or your school's preferred mode of communication can build a transparent and collaborative approach to belonging and brave conversations across the school too.

TIP

Many, many schools use Microsoft Teams, just like many businesses use chat functions like Slack or Google Chat. Why not create a year group 'brave conversations' chat, where you can drop colleagues a quick note to let them know some of the things that have been coming up in form time that may spill over into lessons. It might just be: *'Quite a few students were talking about*

X today. We had a brief chat about it and I let them know to take the conversations to debate club/form time tomorrow, but just letting you know in case it comes up in lessons.'

If your school has a diversity and inclusion lead, or a belonging lead, it may also be useful to have them as part of this group, as it may inform activities or lessons they would like to put in place to develop the culture of belonging at school. They may also notice a pattern if the topic or issue is being discussed and shared across year groups. There is no 'one-size-fits-all' approach to communication; however, when it comes to brave conversations, which are often about challenging topics, it helps to create a collaborative and supportive approach with colleagues.

Having a brave conversation

We can do this in several ways, and you can use all of the strategies below with an entire class or a small group:

- Outline the purpose and aims of the session using contracting (see page 67, Chapter 6). The focus will be on discussing the term 'toxic masculinity' with the students to understand their thoughts and perspectives on the term. We want to engage them in sharing what they think about this concept. How does it make them feel? How do they respond to it?
- You may also want to talk about male role models and social media: who do they follow online and why? Be as clear and transparent as possible so students (and you) know the parameters of the discussion. Outline that this is a safe space where they will not be judged and can speak about their thoughts on masculinity without worrying about the consequences. Ask them for their input too, so that you set boundaries and parameters together – all parties should have ownership and be empowered in the space.
- It is important to emphasise safety and boundaries: if we want students to be honest with us, we must create spaces free of judgement and full of safety for them. In a single-sex school, this may be easier – from speaking to students in mixed schools, boys have told me they are often 'shut down' by girls in the class (and even at home), accused of 'mansplaining' and misogyny. In your class contract, define these terms and make it clear that this is a compassionate space; everyone has different opinions and perspectives, and to reach a space of mutual respect, we need to listen to one another thoroughly before challenging one another (see pages 67-69).

- Once a contract has been set and agreed upon, depending on the relationships and context of the classroom, it may help to lead these sessions with standard classroom practice: guided group discussions with one or two people 'reporting back', or a large class discussion. Your students might feel more comfortable writing down their responses and feelings for you to read later (this can help facilitate a safe space as many students may feel more comfortable with their responses being anonymous). As a teacher, you know your class and students best and therefore you can elicit and maximise honest responses in the best way possible.
- Don't feel you have to respond with an answer or a solution right away. Instead, listen with curiosity and question with curiosity too:
    - *'Help me to understand…'*
    - *'Why do you think that…?'*
    - *'Go on…'* (taken from Simon Sinek's *A Bit of Optimism* podcast!)
    - *'Where does the view/opinion/thought come from?'*

Maintain curiosity and interest over judgement. If other students vehemently agree or disagree, you can continue to use standard behaviour management techniques to remind students about the contract they have agreed to. Curiosity without judgement also works in lessons with unprecedented outbursts or conversations about masculinity (and most themes explored in this book). An outburst may be jarring and uncomfortable, and may not comply with the school's behaviour policy. Remaining calm and composed helps to de-escalate the situation and creates a more conducive environment for productive discussion.

Listening and understanding young people's position is hugely important. If we can amplify their voices *and* gain an understanding of the influences in their lives, we're far more likely to overcome toxic and problematic behaviours associated with, for instance, traditional masculinity.

8 A Values-led School

Creating a values-led classroom and school requires consistent and long-term organisational change and development. While I know, like many teachers, we achieve this on a day-to-day basis in the classroom, to support all teachers, it is an approach that requires the attention and commitment of all stakeholders, particularly senior stakeholders. I now work with schools and senior management in different ways to support them to nurture an inclusive, values-led school. Belonging and connection are not an overnight process; however, with a school-wide, community-led approach, you will start seeing and *feeling* its impact sooner than you think.

I want to take time to discuss a values-led school because, while this book focuses on the classroom, creating a sustainable sense of belonging and connection for every student who walks through your doors requires the whole organisation to be committed to authentic and inclusive values too. Plus, if school values are as clear and blatant as awarding and attainment, it makes the life of a teacher a lot easier!

Reflect on your mission statement

Most schools have a mission statement which often features in open evening speeches, displays and on letterheads. It is important to critically reflect and interrogate the mission statement, particularly for its inclusive values:

- Do the words used in your statement reflect the diverse student body? Can all communities see themselves in it?
- Does the language celebrate authenticity and diversity? Does it encourage young people to work towards their individual strengths, or strive for a particular version of excellence and perfection?
- Is there a balance of masculine, feminine and neutral language?
- Does it make all young people feel safe and connected?
- Does it reflect a school the students are proud of?
- Does it provide a sense of direction for students beyond the school gates?

Research your mission statement

Creating a meaningful mission statement requires input and commitment from the entire school community. It shouldn't be crafted in isolation, but through collaborative research that captures the collective vision and values. Engage stakeholders through focus groups, surveys and open conversations to ensure the mission statement genuinely reflects the school's identity, aspirations, and the community's shared goals. This inclusive approach increases buy-in, making the mission statement more than just words – it becomes a shared commitment to the school's purpose and direction.

Here are some questions you can ask students and staff to build a values-focused mission statement:

1. What is important for a school to offer its staff and/students?
2. What do you want from school?
3. Why did you choose this school? *(perhaps appropriate for staff and parents)*
4. What do you enjoy about school? What do you *not* enjoy?
5. Why is school important to you?
6. When you leave school, what do you want to be remembered for?
7. How would you like to remember your time at school?
8. Name a few things that school does which you think it doesn't need to do.
9. Name a few things that school does which you think are important.
10. Name a few things that school does *not* do, but you think it should.

This list is not exhaustive and can also be adapted and asked in a survey. The key is not to make it so specific to existing school functions. Keep it open and curious, as that way, you are more likely to find out what students and staff value – and that in itself is 'buy in'.

No one wants to fill out a mile-long survey. Use clear and simple language that everyone can easily understand. You could even consider offering a small incentive, like a raffle ticket or a small prize. Share the survey in the school newsletter, announce it during assemblies, and even put up posters around the school. Most importantly, make sure everyone feels comfortable sharing their honest opinions. Let them know that their responses will be anonymous and that their feedback truly matters.

Try different approaches, like focus groups or casual conversations, to get a broader range of perspectives, or try to offer the survey in different languages that parents or carers may speak. And finally, don't keep the results a secret! Share the findings with the whole school community. This shows that you're serious about listening to their input and building a school that reflects their values.

Developing a comprehensive understanding of belonging requires input from diverse stakeholders. Engage teachers, students, parents, local community members, and alumni to gather varied perspectives. Critically, prioritise hearing from minoritised and often marginalised communities whose voices are typically overlooked.

- Who feels a strong sense of belonging in the school?
- Which communities experience a lack of connection?
- What does belonging mean to different groups?
- Who did not or chose not to participate in the discussion?

The insights gained, especially from those who did *not* engage, provide crucial action points for your school development plan. Reverse mentoring (see Chapter 13) can be an effective strategy to uncover deeper insights and create a more inclusive environment.

It is important to focus on student voice when considering the mission statement. After all, your students are your *why* and your main 'customer', therefore it is imperative to engage students, first and foremost. Engage every community, including racialised communities, disabled communities, neurodiverse communities, LGBTQ+ communities, White cis male and female communities (those racially classified as white whose gender identity matches the sex assigned at birth), religious communities, and students with intersectional lived experiences.

I have been challenged by some schools who say this is tokenistic and merely platforms underrepresented voices, as opposed to creating sustainable change. My response to this is that it is always a reflection of school culture. If a school is transparent about their aims, and then goes on to make conscious changes and developments (reverse mentoring can support with this, see Chapter 13), not only are you platforming student voice, but you are listening to influence change and the school culture. If students can see this, they are more likely to engage in feedback. For example, following the advice in this book, you may have affinity groups and societies for underrepresented communities, just like workplaces have staff networks. You can ask these groups and societies for their feedback. Usually, students attend these groups to be with like-minded people and to be in a forum where they can safely express themselves. If you ask the group to provide you with feedback collectively, and you *go to the group* to request it, as opposed to expecting the group to come to you, you are more likely to receive meaningful feedback.

A challenge I often pose to schools, who say it doesn't create sustainable change, is that the latter is not the role of feedback. It is a school's responsibility, specifically a teacher or a senior leader's responsibility, to listen and create meaningful change. If answers and solutions are sought from students or minoritised communities, it may be that you are exploiting student voice or minoritised staff voices, instead of removing barriers and creating meaningful change for the school.

Research conducted in focus groups and via anonymous surveys or feedback forums can also provide a safe platform for minoritised communities that may be less likely to express their views openly and willingly out of fear of being 'excluded' and, very sadly, they may think no one believes them. However, the school 'belongs' to everyone and therefore the views of all staff and students, particularly minoritised students, need to be taken into consideration.

Centre student and staff voices when building a values-led classroom and school. Encourage students and staff to be part of this process so you gain a better understanding of what your community wants from school and why they are a part of your school community too.

Improving engagement requires strategic planning. Consider holding focus groups during lunchtime and providing snacks to encourage participation. For anonymous surveys, using form time can be effective. When leading equality and diversity at a secondary school, I found that booking computer rooms during form time allowed students to complete surveys conveniently. We supported this approach by sending weekly emails to students, and letters to parents, explaining the survey's purpose: to create a safe and inclusive culture by hearing directly from students. This method resulted in responses from nearly two-thirds of the school. Importantly, the process also revealed which groups were not participating, providing valuable insights for future strategic planning. The key is to make participation accessible, meaningful, and demonstrate that every student's voice matters.

RESPONDING TO FEEDBACK

The most important skill for senior leadership at this stage is to listen openly, and without any 'yes but...' responses.

What's a 'yes, but…' response?

A 'yes, but…' response, while well meaning, lacks an understanding of, and empathy for, the person talking or sharing their feelings. These conversations usually follow a pattern, where the 'listener' will nod along, listen, and as soon as they hear something they dislike or disagree with, they will quickly pivot to reiterate a justification, counterargument or their bias, without pausing to consider the views being expressed.

To actively listen and avoid 'yes, but…' responses, it is important to take a deep breath and let everything go, including any predispositions, defences or justifications. It is important to remind yourself that, while you may be 'hearing' complaints and problems, every stakeholder is around the table with a shared purpose: to create an inclusive and connected, values-led school. I fully acknowledge that this is really difficult to do. It requires a culture of 'go on' as Simon Sinek says. It requires minimal senior leader and teacher interjections, but maximum senior leader engagement, compassion and influence. Instead, it will help to frame these feedback and meetings as *research*.

When conducting research, you will look to analyse trends:

- Who is saying what? Who *isn't* saying what?
- What are common and uncommon pieces of qualitative responses?
- How do these responses compare to previous responses and trends?

If you frame staff, student and community feedback as research, it can also encourage stakeholders to be more honest. As opposed to sending out your regular staff, student or parent survey, frame this research as information that will support a culture of inclusion and belonging at our school. As a school, host focus groups, one-on-one meetings and snapshot surveys. These can be led by different people across the school (including students, perhaps Sixth Form students). By framing feedback and surveys as research, you can also critically engage in the information you collect, as opposed to seeing it as something you have to justify and explain.

It is entirely possible to disagree with student and teacher voice and to be saddened, or (pleasantly) surprised, by what you hear and see, too. It is entirely possible that you do not like what they are saying or they share something you've 'never heard' or experienced and witnessed before. This is a good thing because what it means is that staff feel somewhat comfortable sharing negative and constructive experiences with you, giving you an opportunity to nurture the culture of belonging your school desires.

'Yes, but the majority of our students don't feel that way.'

The likelihood is this may be true. However, if students from minoritised backgrounds feel a lack of belonging and connection (and this includes students from low socioeconomic backgrounds and students who have intersectional identities too), your school is only inclusive of the majority and does not have space for minoritised students to be their authentic selves. This is an uncomfortable truth; however, it is a challenge for all teachers and staff to critically consider. Equally, if changes are needed, a deficit narrative is often applied: *'If we make changes for* these *students,* all *students will be asking for what they want too.'* My response to this is usually, why is this a problem? If students see and feel they are being listened to, surely this can only be a good thing, if more students are coming forward in the hope of being heard. While difficult in the moment, I encourage all schools to embrace this as it means you're doing the right thing – you're creating a school where students feel safe to express their thoughts and needs, because they know you will respond.

Values that may emerge

Below you will find a list of inclusive words and phrases that may come out of a school survey, when asking students and staff about values, feelings and characteristics that are important to them at school and beyond. Again, it is not exhaustive and purposefully so: your school values are unique to you and can be phrased and formed in a multitude of ways.

INTEGRITY
TRUST
HONESTY
SAFETY
WELL
CONFIDENT
JOY
AUTHENTICITY
BELONGING
RESILIENCE
PATIENCE
KINDNESS
COLLABORATION
SUPPORT
ALLYSHIP
ANTI-RACISM
JUSTICE

An effective mission statement

Rachel, a retired Headteacher, created the mission 'Dare to Be Remarkable' through an inclusive consultation process. She facilitated workshops with governors, teachers, students and community members, using sticky notes to capture insights. Participants were asked to share what was great about the school, identify barriers, and imagine transformative changes using the prompt: 'If you had a magic wand, what would you change?'

By collating responses into colour-coded columns, Rachel ensured everyone could see their contributions, which would inform the school development plan. These in-person interactions provided qualitative insights often missed in anonymous surveys. She was transparent about the workshops' aim: to improve the school collaboratively, emphasising that the institution belongs to its stakeholders.

The word 'remarkable' held deep significance for Rachel. She wanted every student and staff member to feel valued, whether achieving top grades or simply maintaining consistent attendance. The mission encouraged individuals to embrace their unique strengths, aspirations and potential.

To bring the mission to life, Rachel and her team integrated it comprehensively. The deputy head, Tina, developed the 'Getting Life Ready' (GLR) curriculum around four core values – the 4Rs: Respect for self, others, the environment, and learning. The mission became a 'golden thread' woven through every aspect of school life: parent communications, feedback, recruitment and the house system. Staff intentionally incorporated 'remarkable' into everyday conversations, classroom interactions and school displays. However, Rachel and Tina emphasised that embedding a mission statement is an ongoing process. It requires continuous development to ensure every community member feels recognised and appreciated.

When I led Equity, Diversity, and Inclusion (EDI) at the school, we expanded the mission further. We encouraged students to complete the phrase 'Dare to be... what you want to be', empowering them to personalise the mission and reinforce their sense of belonging.

The journey wasn't without challenges. Rachel nurtured a culture of transparency, welcoming all perspectives – positive, constructive, and critical. Through staff surveys, workshops and feedback sessions, she continuously refined the school's approach.

Ultimately, 'Dare to Be Remarkable' transcended a simple statement. It became a living brand that every student and staff member could identify with and embody throughout their school experience.

Mission statements can change

Like the example from Rachel and Tina, a mission statement can be adapted or changed over time too, to grow and develop with the school. Of course, not every year, but given the rampant changes in education and even within the workforce, staff and student turnover, it might be that the mission statement is revisited with every school development plan and with a little more… feedback.

Recognising values in secondary school

Reward charts and value recognition are also common in the primary school classroom. Several primary schools reward young children for values such as patience, kindness, resilience, hard work, respect and responsibility. I'm not sure why this 'stops' in secondary schools, given when several of us reach the workplace, we find ourselves again looking for recognition and often find 'employee of the week' initiatives and more? Perhaps if we were to continue some of these practices into secondary education, we would find that students maintained a sense of connection with their schools and, given the teenage years are hormonal and tumultuous at the best of times, a values-led reward and recognition approach may provide the anchor and direction students need during these pivotal years.

9 A Values-led Classroom

A successful, values-led school paves the way for a values-led classroom. But, the power and influence of bringing values to life still remains in the hands of the teachers (you), to create a classroom that connects every student, no matter their background or lived experience. Of course, leadership is extremely important in enabling and creating a culture of belonging, however, it is the classroom teacher that can sustainably and authentically nurture feelings of belonging on a daily basis, for every student.

If you are finding that you are working at a school where the senior leadership team or the mission statement and values do not represent inclusion, diversity and belonging, initiate a conversation with your senior leadership team about the power of belonging in your classroom. Prepare a proposal with evidence of the difference it has made to your students, to different groups and demographics of students. You can propose taking a collaborative approach to developing an inclusive mission statement and values-led school, like the case study on page 89. In fact, feel free to hand them a copy of this book and, if you can, offer to support and lead on the work too!

Creating a values-led classroom

Once your school mission statement is on its way, you can start integrating these values into your classroom, along with developing and aligning them with your students' needs. It may be that you don't feel that the school's mission statement *is* inclusive of all students, or that the school is even attempting to alter its mission statement and vision. While addressing this issue can be challenging and may not be something you want to discuss at school, it is crucial to recognise the paradox of belonging and teaching. Teaching is a purposeful and meaningful profession, and I would argue that it is one of the most enjoyable jobs out there. However, this enjoyment can sometimes conflict with the environment of the school you are working in. It may be that as a teacher, you feel that every student is included and belongs in your classroom (and they feel that they belong to your classroom, too), but you don't necessarily find a consistent or mutual sense of inclusion and belonging in the school's broader vision and mission statement. In these situations, it is important to be mindful of your own wellbeing as a teacher and to create a positive, values-led classroom for you and your students.

This book is predominantly about belonging in *your* classroom. Therefore, you are encouraged to use the information in this book to empower yourself as a teacher and to build belonging in *your* classroom. It is where you and your students spend a great deal of time. It is also the space in school where you have the most influence. While a whole-school vision and mission statement are important, as a classroom teacher you can still feel empowered to nurture a culture of belonging and inclusion for your students within the classroom space.

When students know what you as their teacher value, they connect with that, too. As well as respect and manners, it might be timeliness, tidiness, healthy living or exercise. To create a culture of belonging, students must see their teacher as more than just their 'teacher'. They need to see you as an individual and that way, we can see our students as individuals too.

During a lesson, particularly at the beginning of the school year, call out examples of students modelling your class values. Make it clear to everyone in the classroom that these values are celebrated and lead to every student's success. Think DNE:

1 **Describe** what the student did.

2 **Name** the value.

3 **Explain** why it matters.

Here are some examples of value-led feedback that you could base your DNE comments on:

VALUE	FEEDBACK
collaboration	*'It was great seeing you working collaboratively when you supported your partner/group. We value collaboration in this classroom and school because it leads to everyone's success.'*
anti-racism	*'When we were talking about migration, and some students kept using the words 'foreigners' and 'Browns and Blacks', you interjected politely and said we should use the word 'migrant', or refer to their heritage. You also briefly expressed how those words can be offensive and that people are not just colours. We really value this example of anti-racism in the classroom, and your confidence to say this with maturity to your fellow students encouraged students to listen and acknowledge their use of language.'*

VALUE	FEEDBACK
safety	*'It was lovely to see you supporting a younger student who came to our classroom feeling lost and you offered to take them to their class. You smiled at them and said you're happy to help, which made them feel safe, something we really value here. It helps that students know they can always ask for help at this school without feeling too vulnerable.'*

These are just a few examples and can be adapted to suit your students and class environment. It can help to say these out loud in front of your class to model the values and expectations for the class. For Key Stage 3, adopt a routine of value recognition at the end of the week or during a specific lesson. This doesn't need to take more than ten minutes of a lesson or out of your week, but the positive impact can be significant for the whole class and, hopefully, infectious too. You could create signage or posters for the classroom to highlight value-led behaviours. This doesn't have to occur at a fixed time and can be flexible, but you can then use these materials to point out a specific value-led behaviour as an example for the rest of the class. You can ask students to point these out, too, particularly for Years 7 and 8 students, who may be used to this type of routine from primary school where values such as kindness, resilience and sharing are acknowledged.

Encouraging connection, respect and manners in the classroom

Celebrate the values that students exhibit in your classroom. Praise students for their behaviour and connection to your classroom and model this in front of them to create a positive learning environment for all students.

CASE STUDY

Value-led recognition with Year 9

Several years ago, during my NQT year (what would now be the first ECT year), I was given two Year 9 classes that I found very challenging to teach for many reasons. I often left lessons in tears and was advised to focus on making lessons more engaging; observations focused on different learning styles, even though I'd consistently achieved 'good' and 'outstanding' for my observation lessons. I realised my issues were not with their learning or my teaching but with their behaviour. It was with the lack of connection they had with *my* classroom and it was the lack of connection they had with one another and with *me.* After all, physical connection and belonging in the classroom space are so important, given teaching is face to face (even in a post-Covid environment) and as teachers, we want to ensure students feel comfortable and connected walking into their learning environments. It got to a point where I considered leaving the job before my NQT year was up.

I remember creating a reward chart for each class one weekend, wanting to show them what mattered most: manners and respect in the classroom. At the time, based on my experiences with the classes, this included things like greeting one another upon entering the classroom, raising hands to contribute and not calling out, out of respect for one another's learning (the classes were mixed ability with a range of individual needs). It also included talking respectfully to one another, including me as a teacher. For one class, it included communicating with kindness and a smile – I wanted English lessons to be a place where they all felt comfortable and safe, and while they may not always find the subject matter interesting, I wanted them to enjoy elements of every lesson.

The following week, they all walked in, and I was brutally honest and vulnerable with them for the first time. I explained how they had been making me feel and how I wanted us to get along, enjoy the lessons and enjoy each other's company for the three hours a week I saw them. I spent about 15 minutes reintroducing myself and asked each of them to reintroduce themselves and share something about themselves that I didn't know. I also asked them for their views and input on my explanations of manners and respect, and no one had any objections or additions. This was my first real experience in contracting. I also shook each class member's hand, which was funny, and they found it a little awkward, I'm sure, but they all complied.

They then saw the reward chart and I explained that for every lesson where I felt they'd exhibited manners and respect as explained above, they would be rewarded with a star. I was very aware that these were 14-year-old teenagers, so they may well have just laughed in my face. As a teacher, particularly a new teacher, I was putting myself in a very vulnerable position. But, luckily for me, they absolutely loved it.

Every week for nearly the whole year, they competed for their stars and the competition it inspired in the classroom was genuinely heart-warming and hilarious. They would rush to raise their hands to answer questions, and make it so obvious they were working collaboratively and supporting one another as I walked around the classroom – it created such a warm and fun atmosphere. The stars were not associated with their grades, attainment or progress; just with respect and manners. The cheeky sweet at the end of the week was an incentive too. Of course, sweets and rewards are not what I am advising here; they just worked for me at the time, and I encourage teachers to trust their instincts and develop an approach like this that works for you and your students. After all, you know your students best.

Is this 'intervention' groundbreakingly innovative? No, not really. However, years later I realised it worked so successfully because it encouraged the students to connect with each other and with me as human beings. We connected through a mutual understanding and communication about manners and respect, values and behaviours, that positively impacted them and me as their teacher. Not everything was about English or their progress and attainment. Instead, I explicitly verbalised that I wanted to connect with them, and I wanted us to get along and enjoy our lessons together – it brought out the best in me and them. It led me to realise that another value was significant to me, too: joy in the classroom.

The lesson in belonging and connection here is that being vulnerable in my classroom did not necessarily mean feeling unsafe or uncomfortable. In fact, it meant being honest, transparent and communicating what I wanted *our* classroom to be and feel like. It was also the first time I had formally used a form of contracting to define manners and respect. Equally, it led to joy, which soon became another value I wanted to incorporate into my classroom.

The difference a values-led classroom makes

Of course, a values-led classroom is part of a 'bigger picture' and by no means is a 'happily ever after' to the perfect classroom. However, studies have shown that nurturing values-led classrooms, celebrating and recognising values, belonging and connection can improve the success and achievement of all students in the classroom.[17]

In his book *Belonging*, Cohen recounts walking his daughter to a new school, feeing apprehensive and nervous. However, she was simply approached by an older student with enthusiasm and connection: the older student sharing that they too had attended the same previous school and both engaged in a great conversation. Before he knew it, his daughter happily walked into school without looking back.[18]

Cohen emphasises that the values of inclusion and respect and 'wise interventions' that build confidence and belonging in the classroom lead to high achievement for all. One such study he highlights is when vulnerable students were tasked with completing 'values-affirmation' activities. The intervention was successful and

[17] G. L. Cohen, *Belonging: The Science of Creating Connection and Building Trust*, New York, W. W. Norton & Company, 2022, pp. 211–17.

[18] G. L. Cohen, *Belonging: The Science of Creating Connection and Building Trust*, New York, W. W. Norton & Company, 2022, p. 211.

infectious: all students completed it and the teachers were able to focus on teaching, learning and achievement more than having to focus on students at risk of failing.[19]

Helping students to find connection

Nurturing a culture of belonging, connecting with every student and having a shared set of values, particularly in a secondary school setting, where we see students develop and grow into young adults, is what I loved about teaching and being in the classroom, and what I have tried to recreate through the *School Should Be...* blog and podcast, and now this book.

When teaching and leading a core subject, the purpose was of course for students to 'engage' in the curriculum and enjoy my lessons, but it would be disingenuous not to admit that the predominant purpose was awarding and attainment. Between the laughter and joy with students, they knew they were there to achieve a grade; a grade that would likely get them to their next step, whether that was work, A levels or university.

Let me begin by saying that there is nothing wrong with that. I know my students appreciated the focus on their academic success and the countless practice essays teachers mark and work through with them. However, I often remember my conversations with students who felt a little lost and disempowered by the system, and while their 'next steps' were clear, they lacked a sense of direction. It also revealed that my students felt safe, comfortable, and able to be truthful and honest with me (a sense of belonging in the classroom) – even if they felt conflicted with the school and education system. It is important to remember that belonging and connection does not mean we all have the same feelings as one another in the classroom. Instead, belonging and connection with the classroom and school mean that students feel safe to be honest and authentic, too.

Aaron was brilliant in every way possible. He worked extremely hard, achieved excellent grades and excelled in extracurricular activities. Aaron was a model student. I taught him for nearly five years, and I still remember an occasion in Year 8 when he knocked on the office door and handed in his homework two days before it was due because he wasn't going to be in school for our upcoming lesson (for another extracurricular-related project). To say I envied his organisational skills is an understatement. However, in Year 13, I remember a few conversations with Aaron where he explained feeling disillusioned and disconnected from school and education in general. He had lost his motivation and his sense of purpose. A high-achieving

[19]G. L. Cohen, *Belonging: The Science of Creating Connection and Building Trust*, New York, W. W. Norton & Company, 2022, p. 215.

student, the world his oyster and Aaron feels lost? I thought to myself, if Aaron feels like this, imagine how many other students must feel the same too? On the one hand, I was grateful that Aaron had confided in me; on the other, I was concerned about what we were doing in school and education at large that was causing this disconnect.

Since starting the *School Should Be...* podcast, and speaking to many students, it seems, while conversations in the classroom with teachers reinforced feelings of belonging and connection, they did not necessarily trump awarding and attainment. While the latter is an important and primary function of schooling, there needs to be a consistent focus on values and attributes that students can identify and connect with, to take forward in their future lives. If they leave school and 'fly the nest' they once belonged to, we must make sure they fly high with direction and purpose. There is a distinction between feeling lost and being curious. It is perfectly acceptable for young people to leave school without a clear vision or plan, as long as they possess the skills and support needed to explore and be adventurous. This journey of curiosity will help them to discover their interests, identify their goals, and determine what they want to prioritise for their futures.

While I did not have an answer for Aaron then (and, as a teacher, I was so determined to provide a solution), I have kept in touch with him over the years, which included recording a podcast with him about wellbeing. He has intentionally taken steps to self-reflect, be present, and be kind to himself so that he can find his way. Often, compared to grades, it is our relationship with students which has a meaningful impact. Of course that journey is not finite and is a lifetime of discovery.

However, we want young people to leave feeling connected to the values they have learned at school, rather than feeling lost after everything they have accomplished. My purpose in including Aaron's story is to show that belonging and connection in the classroom go beyond what we might expect of the classroom, and beyond just teaching schemes of work and helping students to achieve grades and do well at school.

10 Safeguarding and Allyship

What is allyship?

Author and coach Hira Ali focuses particularly on allyship for women. In her book *Her Allies*, Ali defines allyship as a commitment to supporting, understanding, sponsoring and advocating for women; she explains that an ally will commit to improving their self-awareness so that they can be a 'catalyst for change and become a role model for others'.[20] Ali also makes the important point that allyship is not heroic nor should it come across as patronising or 'all knowing'. Instead, allies need to continue learning and working side by side with minoritised students and staff, which can be achieved in a range of ways from advocacy, sponsorship to coaching, and mentoring too. Samantha Rae-Dickinson goes further to say, 'allies must also have some degree of power to effect change'.[21]

Allyship in the classroom

In a classroom setting, particularly in an environment where students are learning to collaborate, advocate for themselves and others, develop skills of curiosity and understand more about their own identities, every student is an ally. Every student has the ability to influence and effect change, particularly when this concerns supporting their classmates and those vulnerable to prejudice, racism, bias, homophobia, transphobia, sexism, Islamophobia, antisemitism, disability discrimination, and so much more. From a student's perspective, the discrimination they see and experience in the classroom may be regarded as nothing more than 'banter' or a 'joke'; in these situations, showing up as an ally is even more important.

A teacher is also an ally in every classroom and has a responsibility to ally with every student. There is an additional layer of responsibility for a teacher as an ally, and that is the responsibility of safeguarding. DEIJB is a safeguarding concern, and to keep children safe, teachers must use their power and position in the classroom to support every student. While building trust, belonging, safety and joy in the classroom, allyship can also support student attainment and confidence in the classroom. As with every classroom skill, allyship requires preparation, learning and practice and, to reassure

[20]H. Ali, *Her Allies: A Practical Toolkit to Help Men Lead Through Advocacy*, Neem Tree Press, 2021, p. 12.
[21]www.edi.nih.gov/blog/communities/what-allyship – accessed 3 May 2024

teachers reading this book, it does not need to be an overwhelming or a daunting practice. Allyship is learned and an integral part of allyship is learning.

Challenges of allyship

'It just doesn't work in practice.'

Every teacher I have spoken to has commented that while allyship is absolutely necessary in the classroom, it doesn't always work in practice, particularly when things are said 'in the moment'. Students have diverse (and in many cases) opposing opinions and there just isn't enough time to fully address the positives or problems of what is 'called out' and 'called in' in a classroom. Equally, if there are feelings of uncertainty about what is being discussed, particularly when it comes to race, religion, disability, sexuality and gender, it is entirely understandable why teachers (and also students and parents) may not want to engage.

To overcome the fear or discomfort associated with allyship in the classroom, it can help to reframe allyship as safeguarding for students. This is something deeply rooted in teaching, and every teacher will want to safeguard every student in their care. If we reframe allyship as safeguarding or see it as an intrinsic part of safeguarding, we are likely to grow and feel more confident with acts of allyship too.

Teaching anti-racism and allyship

Nurturing a culture of belonging in our classrooms is social justice in action. To teach anti-racism and allyship in the classroom so that our students ally with the LGBTQ+ community, neurodivergent communities, disabled communities, religious communities, disadvantaged communities and more (intersectional identities), is social justice in action. Most importantly, by integrating these practices into everyday classroom activities and discussions, we create a sustainable culture of respect, dignity and inclusion for every student.

Calling out discriminatory behaviour

This does not mean we can't call out or address behaviour that is discriminatory and/or problematic for other students. Discipline is imperative in an inclusive classroom, particularly discipline that creates a respectful and fair environment for all students.

Boys as young as 12 have said they know what the right thing to do is (call it out or report it), but out of fear of belonging and fitting in, they choose to say nothing or laugh along with 'the joke', no matter what the joke is. Some students have said that while the classroom is not perfect, they still feel safest in the classroom where there are boundaries; in the school playground and the comment sections on social media, there are limited parameters in which to feel secure. We must teach and model positive behaviour in the classroom, but it is equally imperative that we empower young people to confidently and safely address problematic behaviours.

Students have commented that this isn't necessarily the sole responsibility of the teacher. Instead, they have recommended some strategies for fellow students:

- Address problematic behaviour on a one-to-one basis. Take the friend or peer acting problematically and talk to them. Use phrases such as:
    - *'Just wondering what you meant when you said...?'*
    - *'I don't know if you're aware, but that is offensive, disrespectful towards...'*
    - *'I know you say it's banter, and I get it, we all like a laugh from time to time, but it's not OK...'*
- Don't laugh. Simply unacknowledging, not laughing at the 'sexist joke' or stepping away from the situation can be powerful. Of course, this can still be very overwhelming and difficult for students, which is why a transparent school charter and behaviour policy which protects allies and victims, and holds perpetrators accountable (through conversation and discussions, not necessarily sanctions) is very important to create a culture of safety, bravery and belonging for all.
- Are you OK? Check in on the victim. Sometimes, instead of calling it out, it can help to support the victim of bullying and harassment by checking in on them. Students said that if we give victims confidence to know the behaviour isn't OK, they are more likely to report it.

Teenagers have said that it's not so much the fear factor, but they don't know 'what to say' and don't want to be 'the one to call out' a friend or classmate. Interestingly, saying nothing can also harm a student's or teacher's sense of belonging. Confidence, skills and 'knowing what to say' in order to have uncomfortable conversations have, by far, been the most common requests in DEIJB training. Staff and students alike are actively looking for concrete strategies for navigating challenging conversations, including how to respond to microaggressions, how to address bias, and how to engage in respectful dialogue across differences.

Engaging in these critical conversations, particularly on a day-to-day basis in a place where students find themselves most often, with people they see more than anyone else during their teenage years, is a core part of allyship and can help to develop trust and positive relationships in the classroom: key aspects of creating belonging in the classroom.

Raising awareness

A student I worked with, named Aleena, had a rare, hidden disability. She came to me wanting to create awareness about her condition through her EPQ project, a 5000-word independent essay or project students can undertake at A level on a topic of their choice. Aleena decided to record a podcast with me about her disability, write a blog, and host a whole-year group awareness event with guest speakers to talk about hidden disabilities like hers. She also recorded a 30-minute CPD webinar for teachers, which we could share with staff across the school. A few months ago, Aleena got back in touch with me and also with the Pituitary Foundation. She asked if I would record a webinar with her and the foundation for parents supporting their children with conditions like hers.

Working with Aleena was a learning experience for me as I had not heard of her hidden disability before. However, in my role of creating awareness around the school about belonging and inclusion, we found avenues and opportunities for allyship in action with such impactful outcomes.

Aleena's initiative exemplifies the power of student voice and agency in fostering a more inclusive and understanding school environment. Aleena wanted to share her lived experiences and used a school-based project, something that was part of her timetable and school commitments, to do just this. As a teacher, we can empower students to share their experiences and become advocates for themselves and others. Just like in Aleena's case, her fellow students responded warmly and positively to her impactful role modelling of sharing lived experiences in a professional and safe way.

11 Curriculum Reform

A truly diverse curriculum goes beyond simply including different voices; it ensures that these perspectives shape the entire learning experience. This means critically examining existing curriculum materials to identify and address any gaps or biases.

For example, we need to ensure that the curriculum accurately and fairly represents the contributions of Black, Asian and global majority heritage (often racialised as 'other' or 'diverse') individuals across all subjects. This involves:

- **Identifying and addressing omissions:** recognising and rectifying instances where the contributions of racialised individuals are overlooked or marginalised.
- **Challenging stereotypes:** examining and challenging any stereotypes or misrepresentations of global majority communities within the curriculum.
- **Incorporating diverse and different perspectives:** actively seeking out and incorporating a range of voices, experiences and perspectives from different, particularly minoritised and underrepresented, communities into all aspects of the curriculum.

While I'm using global majority students as an example here, of course these principles apply to any kind of protected characteristic: sex, ethnicity, race, gender, socioeconomic class, etc.

An underrepresented and disconnected curriculum

According to Pearson's Diversity and Inclusion in Schools Report (2019), 26 per cent of teaching staff already feel that the education provided in schools today does not reflect the diversity of the pupils in their classrooms. Interestingly, this figure increased to 32 per cent (one in three teaching staff) in 2020, which is perhaps in light of our raised consciousness and awareness of inequality and racism. The murder of George Floyd glaringly revealed how so many of us were oblivious to inequality, injustice, discrimination, racism, and so much more. It has since led to so many reports, research, individuals and organisations sharing their experiences of inequality and a lack of belonging, particularly in institutions like education.[22] The research also found that over

[22]More animal main characters than non-white people in children's books - CBBC Newsround. (n.d.). www.bbc.co.uk. [online] Available at: www.bbc.co.uk/newsround/54900501.

50 per cent of teachers think LGBTQ+ and non-binary groups are underrepresented in teaching materials. Over 30 per cent of educators feel the same way about representing special education needs, disabilities, and disadvantaged pupils.

Students need to see themselves reflected in the books they read. However, many school curriculums don't include enough works by Black, Asian, and minority ethnic writers, even though these writers make significant contributions to British literature. Children's books are eight times more likely to feature an animal than a non-white person in the lead role.[23]

A report commissioned by think tank The Runnymede Trust found that:

- At most, 7 per cent of students in England studied a text by a woman for their English literature GCSE, and just 0.1 per cent a text by a woman of colour. Fewer than 1 per cent of candidates for GCSE English Literature in 2019 answered a question on a novel by an author of colour.
- 82 per cent of youth survey respondents did not recall ever studying a text by a Black, Asian or minority ethnic author.
- The teaching profession in England is overwhelmingly white, and there is evidence that teachers of English have even lower levels of ethnic diversity.
- The greatest obstacles to teaching more diverse texts are time, money, subject knowledge and teacher confidence.[24]

We all know that if our curriculum only shows one side of the story, we're doing our students a disservice. That's why curriculum reform is absolutely crucial. A big part of this is us, as teachers, taking a good hard look at our own materials – textbooks, lesson plans, the whole lot. We need to dig deep and spot any biases, places where important voices are missing, and any lack of diversity. Once we've identified those gaps, we can push for more inclusive curriculum options and create awesome resources that truly centre the experiences of all our students. This isn't just about making things 'fair'; it's about creating a richer learning experience for everyone and building a classroom where every student feels seen and valued.

What is an audit?

Curriculum audits help us to understand how well our teaching and learning are actually working. They involve carefully examining what we teach, how we teach it, and whether students are truly gaining the knowledge, skills and mindset they

[23]Lit-in-Colour-research-report.pdf
[24]Lit-in-Colour-research-report.pdf

need to succeed. Schools can choose to conduct these audits themselves, using the expertise of their own staff. Alternatively, they can bring in outside experts for a more independent and objective view. While internal audits can be more cost-effective and offer valuable insights into the unique challenges of a particular school, external audits can provide a fresh perspective and help to ensure a fair and unbiased assessment.

Thinking about diversity audits can feel overwhelming, but breaking them down can make the process more manageable. We can start by considering four key areas: ***diversity***, ***inclusion***, ***equity*** and ***justice***. A diversity audit might focus on representation, ensuring that the curriculum includes diverse voices, perspectives and experiences. An inclusion audit would then examine how well these diverse voices are integrated and whether all students feel a sense of belonging in the classroom. An equity audit would investigate whether all students have equal access to resources and opportunities to succeed, regardless of their background. Finally, a justice audit would delve deeper, examining how the curriculum and school systems may perpetuate systemic inequalities, and explore ways to dismantle those systems.

Diversity

The diversity audit primarily focuses on representation, looking at your curriculum and resources to identify and address gaps in the inclusion of diverse perspectives, authors and experiences. However, a diversity audit isn't just about counting how many women or people of colour are on your syllabus. It's about examining whose voices are truly heard and whose stories are being told.

TIP

Consider: Who gets to decide which perspectives are 'diverse' enough? When we only include a token few authors from marginalised groups, are we truly addressing power imbalances? If your English class primarily reads white male authors, with one exception being Meera Syal's *Anita and Me* at the very end, that's a step in the right direction, but it still reinforces a certain hierarchy. If you are looking at urbanisation in Geography, be weary of generalisations made about 'who' lives in urban areas and 'why' they live there. Nuance and addressing deficit narratives is very important when creating a diverse curriculum. As well as offering diverse content, you want to offer diverse perspectives too.

A truly diverse curriculum reflects the full spectrum of human experience. It considers not just race and gender, but also class, sexuality, disability, and countless other intersections. It would challenge dominant narratives and centre marginalised voices.

Inclusion

Inclusion isn't merely about having a diverse student body in the classroom; it's about fostering an environment where every student feels seen, valued and respected. Rudine Sims Bishop's powerful metaphor highlights this: students need 'mirrors' that reflect their own experiences and 'windows' that offer glimpses into the lives of others.

To identify these 'mirrors' and 'windows', we must actively listen to our students. Which stories resonate with them? What experiences feel absent from their education? Inclusion audits examine whether learners at your school encounter these 'mirrors' and 'windows' within the curriculum. However, a true inclusion audit goes beyond simply adding diverse books, themes and topics. It's about connecting learning to the real world in meaningful ways.

For example, instead of relying solely on newspaper articles for 'current events', consider exploring your local community. Encourage students to interview local leaders, delve into the history of your city, and investigate how local issues connect to global contexts. This approach makes learning relevant and engaging for students, demonstrating how the world around them connects to the bigger picture. A deputy headteacher at one school shared that he was surprised at how little the school community knew about the local area their students lived in and are 'from'. He encouraged teachers to visit the local libraries and to design projects for students, particularly Key Stage 3 students, to explore the local community too. In many ways this is equitable and accessible too, if they are able to walk into their local community to complete homework projects. It also emphasises to students that while we sit in diverse classrooms, we have shared experiences too, something they may not be consciously aware of when they think of the words 'diversity' and 'inclusion'.

True inclusion requires accurate and respectful representation of diverse experiences. Let's consider the Industrial Revolution. While examining the plight of white working-class children in the North of England is crucial, it's equally important to acknowledge the significant impact of the transatlantic slave trade on British industry. Historian Joseph Inikori argues that the profits generated by the slave trade provided crucial capital for the development of British industry during this period. Including this perspective highlights the direct link between the exploitation of enslaved people and the economic advancements that fuelled the Industrial Revolution. Elif Shafak's recent publication, *There Are Rivers in the Sky*, beautifully weaves the epic of Gilgamesh into a narrative about an eighteenth-century boy, raised in the slums of Victorian London, the experiences of a nine-year-old Yazidi girl in 2014, and a twenty-first-century female protagonist who was orphaned as a child. The thread that weaves their narratives together is water, its precious nature and scarcity in the world today: a book filled with extracts that can be explored in English, History, Geography and Politics.

Inclusion also extends beyond the *content* of lessons. How are students engaging with the material? Are they passive recipients of information, or are they actively involved in discovering, creating and sharing knowledge?

An effective inclusion audit goes beyond mere representation; it examines how all students feel included and valued within the learning environment. This may involve conducting student and staff surveys, asking students how they feel in the classroom, and exploring issues of accessibility and equity.

Equity

While diversity audits focus on *who* is represented in the curriculum, equity audits delve deeper, examining how the curriculum serves *all students fairly*. Equity means ensuring that every student has the opportunity to fully engage with the learning process and benefit from their education, without facing undue obstacles.

An equity audit begins by carefully examining how students are expected to interact with the curriculum. What does 'engagement' truly mean in this context? What are the intended learning outcomes, and how can we ensure all students can achieve them?

Crucial questions to ask include:

- Who can fully participate in this learning activity?
- Who can only participate partially?
- Who is excluded entirely?
- Who can easily access the benefits of this learning, and who faces additional burdens in doing so?

For example, consider a seemingly inclusive activity: students are asked to bring in a family recipe that reflects their cultural heritage. While well intentioned, this activity can create unintended barriers. Students from diverse family structures, those experiencing food insecurity, or those with dietary restrictions may face significant challenges in completing the assignment. Instead, it may be that you present a range of recipes or recipe books from different authors and ask students if there are any they recognise, that are familiar, foods they have tried or haven't tried, or any questions they have about certain ingredients. Sometimes, curiosity can create equitable and inclusive classroom experiences, without students feeling any personal pressure (even if well intended).

Equity demands more than simply including diverse content. We must critically examine how our teaching practices might inadvertently create or reinforce existing inequalities. In this example, the teacher could adapt the assignment by allowing students to research a recipe that connects to a personal story, or by collaborating with families to find alternative ways for students to demonstrate their understanding.

Equity audits also examine the broader educational system. Do our lessons or assessments prioritise certain skills or learning styles? What criteria determine access to resources, and whose needs do these criteria ultimately serve?

Finally, an equity audit considers the long-term impact of education. What opportunities will students have to apply their learning beyond the classroom? How can we ensure that all students have the chance to use their knowledge and skills to contribute to their communities and shape their futures?

As the most comprehensive type of audit, equity audits delve deep into systemic issues and potential harms within the curriculum. They require a careful analysis of teaching practices, assessment methods and the overall school climate, in order to identify and address potential biases and inequities.

Justice

True justice involves not only rectifying past wrongs but also actively preventing future harm. It demands the creation of systems that foster healing, belonging and liberation for all. A justice audit prompts critical reflection: How has this curriculum potentially caused harm? How can we hold ourselves accountable and prevent future harm? What innovative approaches can we develop to create a more just and equitable learning environment?

Educators like Stephanie Jones (2020) use the term 'curriculum violence' to describe how insensitive or harmful teaching practices can negatively impact students.[25] This can include minimising or misrepresenting history, perpetuating harmful stereotypes, or creating a climate of exclusion and marginalisation.

While some teachers may resist this terminology, acknowledging the potential for harm within educational systems is crucial. This requires honest self-reflection and a willingness to confront our own biases and the systemic inequalities that may be embedded within our practices.

A true justice audit necessitates a collaborative and community-centred approach. It requires actively involving community members from historically marginalised groups, including students, parents and community leaders. This process may be challenging, but it is essential for creating a truly just and equitable education system for all.

For example, History curricula often heavily emphasise European history and perspectives, neglecting the contributions and experiences of people from other parts of the world. This can reinforce a Eurocentric worldview and marginalise the

---

[25] Ending Curriculum Violence | Learning for Justice

histories and cultures of other communities. It's crucial to explore ways to address this issue beyond the confines of Black History Month, for example.

How do we prepare?

Let's be honest, conducting a DEIJB-based curriculum audit can feel a bit overwhelming, especially if you're doing it on your own. It can be easy to feel daunted by the scale of the task. But remember, this is about making your classroom a more inclusive and equitable space for all your students. And every small step you take makes a difference.

Begin by critically examining your own teaching practices. Scrutinise the materials you use – do they showcase a diverse array of voices and experiences? Are you employing inclusive language while conscientiously avoiding stereotypes? Do your teaching methods cater effectively to the diverse learning styles within your classroom?

Consider these questions:

- **Representation**:
  - Who are the authors and characters featured in your curriculum materials?
  - Are there any noticeable gaps or underrepresentation of specific groups or experiences?
  - Do the materials accurately and respectfully portray diverse cultures and perspectives?
- **Language**:
  - Are you using gender-neutral language whenever possible?
  - Are you mindful of the potential impact of your language choices on students from different backgrounds?
  - Are you avoiding stereotypes and microaggressions, both intentional and unintentional?
- **Teaching methods:**
  - Do your teaching methods cater to a range of learning styles, such as visual, auditory and kinaesthetic learners?
  - Do you provide opportunities for diverse forms of expression, such as creative writing, art and presentations?
  - Are you creating a classroom environment where all students feel comfortable participating and sharing their ideas?

Remember, this is an ongoing process of learning and reflection. There's no need to feel pressured to do everything at once. Start with one small change, such as incorporating a new diverse text into your reading list, or modifying an assignment to be more inclusive. Celebrate your successes and don't be afraid to ask for support from colleagues or mentors. By taking these small steps, you can create a more equitable and inclusive learning experience for all your students.

Auditing your curriculum

So, how do you actually conduct a curriculum audit? Well, first things first, you need a plan! Let's break it down into manageable steps.

- Get organised: You need to make sure you have all the necessary documents – begin with curriculum maps in your subject area. Then you can move on to schemes of work, lesson plans (depending on how your department or team 'does' lesson planning). This will help you get a complete picture.
- Ask yourself:
  1. What story is your curriculum telling?
  2. Who are the main characters, the supporting acts, the 'extras'? Who are the directors and who is in the end credits?
  3. Which topics and content in your schemes and units of work are representative of your students, your school community?
  4. Which units and schemes of work enable diverse, inclusive and equitable learning experiences for them? How?
  5. Is your curriculum representative of the society students are experiencing? Is there a 'shared and equitable cultural capital', or does your curriculum take a predominantly traditionalist and Eurocentric approach to cultural awareness and capital?
  6. How do students feel about what they are learning?
  7. How do you feel about what you are teaching?
  8. What do you want to see more of on your curriculum?
  9. What do you want to see less of on your curriculum?

This is by no means an exhaustive list and you do not need to answer every question. You also do not need to complete this audit in one sitting! It can help to tabularise the questions and make notes for each question against each scheme of work and your curriculum map. You can then add a 'What's next?' box at the end, with agreed actions and a timeframe for you and your colleagues to collectively work together and create a curriculum that represents the culture of inclusion and belonging you wish to create.

Remember, this isn't about finding fault. It's about continuous improvement. By working together and embracing a collaborative approach, we can create a curriculum that best serves the needs of all our students.

What comes next?

Once you've reflected on these areas, consider taking concrete steps, such as exploring valuable resources on inclusive teaching practices, and addressing inequalities in education offered by organisations such as DiverseEd, Bloomsbury, Penguin's 'Lit in Colour' campaign, and Leeds Beckett University's Centre for Race and Decoloniality. Seek out diverse perspectives by exploring a range of resources by authors from diverse backgrounds, using the reading list at the end of this book as a starting point. Engage in professional development opportunities by participating in workshops or courses on DEI in education. Collaborate with colleagues from different departments or year groups in order to discuss your findings and share ideas. Finally, actively seek feedback from your students on their learning experiences to gain valuable insights and perspectives on the changes you've made.

SOME SIMPLE IDEAS

Once you get into this way of thinking, I promise it becomes a lot easier!

SUBJECT	EXAMPLES FOR A DIVERSE CURRICULUM
ENGLISH LITERATURE	• Include works by diverse authors like Malala Yousafzai, Chimamanda Ngozi Adichie, Bernardine Evaristo, Elif Shafak, Malorie Blackman, Bali Rai and Akala. • Explore contemporary poetry forms like spoken word, rap, and slam poetry. • Explore texts from around the world, including works in translation.

SUBJECT	EXAMPLES FOR A DIVERSE CURRICULUM
HISTORY	• Include studies of African, Asian, and Indigenous histories and civilisations. • Explore the complexities and nuances of historical figures, and diverse perspectives on their actions. • Explore social, cultural and economic history, including the experiences of marginalised groups. • Include oral histories and welcome guest speakers to share histories that have been communicated and celebrated using the spoken word.
GEOGRAPHY	• Explore the perspectives of people living in the Global South. • Acknowledge and discuss issues like climate change, inequality and conflict from multiple perspectives. • Use up-to-date and respectful images and descriptions of different cultures.
SCIENCE	• Highlight the contributions of scientists from diverse backgrounds, including women and people of colour. • Discuss the social and ethical implications of scientific discoveries and technologies. • Use examples that are relevant and relatable to all students, regardless of their background.
MATHS	• Use examples that reflect the diversity of human experiences (e.g. diverse family structures). • Connect mathematical concepts to real-world issues and challenges faced by diverse communities. • Encourage projects that look at the origins of mathematics, including mathematical philosophies and numerical communication across the world.
MODERN FOREIGN LANGUAGES	• Explore the diverse cultures and languages within the target language country. • Explore informal language and slang used by young people in the target language country. • Use examples that are relevant and relatable to people from all social and economic backgrounds.

SUBJECT	EXAMPLES FOR A DIVERSE CURRICULUM
ART & DESIGN	• Explore a wide range of art forms from around the world, including Indigenous art, African art and Asian art. • Encourage students to experiment with a variety of media, including digital art, photography and film. • Discuss the social, cultural and political significance of art.
MUSIC	• Explore a wide range of musical genres from around the world, including traditional music, folk music and popular music. • Explore the music of diverse communities, including marginalised and underrepresented groups. • Explore the cultural and social significance of music in different societies.
PE	• Explore a range of physical activities, including dance, yoga, and outdoor activities. • Provide a range of equipment and clothing options to ensure accessibility for all students. • Ensure displays and content are representative of global athletes and share their experiences too, for example, Michael Holding's book, *Why We Kneel, How We Rise*. • Emphasise teamwork, cooperation and inclusivity.
CITIZENSHIP	• Explore the history and culture of diverse communities within the UK and around the world. • Explore issues of social justice, inequality and discrimination. • Explore the role of community action and social movements in creating positive change.

TIP

You can also refer to online groups and blogs, such as 'Learning for Justice', 'The Black Curriculum' and others, for ideas, shared resources and more. Don't feel like you need to research and create everything all by yourself – in fact, the more input from different perspectives and people, the better.

Teachers need (supportive) teaching, too

For decades, educators have advocated for increased representation of Black authors within school literature programmes. The Black Lives Matter movement has encouraged many schools, exam boards and education bodies to reconsider their curriculum choices.

A 2021 Commission on Race and Ethnic Disparities (CRED) report recommended sweeping curriculum reforms to boost the representation of Black, Asian, and minority ethnic communities. The report argued that a more inclusive curriculum, reflecting a wider spectrum of experiences, histories and perspectives, would not only be more engaging for students but also better prepare them for citizenship in our multicultural world.

Pearson Edexcel has recently added more books by diverse authors to their GCSE English Literature options. These include works by Tanika Gupta, Lemn Sissay, Jamila Gavin and Malorie Blackman. OCR has also announced plans to increase the diversity of their texts at GCSE and A Level.

As schools begin to diversify their curriculums and increase representation across the board, teachers must be supported to navigate the conversations and discussions that arise about race, sexuality, identity, religion, masculinity, femininity, class and societal structures – especially as a diversified curriculum will naturally encourage a diversity of thoughts and opinions too.

Recognising this need, publishers and exam boards are striving to bridge this gap. The 'Lit in Colour' project, a collaborative effort between Penguin Books UK and the race equality think tank, The Runnymede Trust, was launched in 2020. Their aim is to support schools in making the teaching and learning of English literature more inclusive. This includes commissioning research to better understand barriers and possible solutions, as well as providing practical support, including book donations and free teaching resources on their website.

The challenges of effective PSHE

Implementing lessons on complex topics such as masculinity, gender equity and feminism is crucial, but they don't always hit the mark in the classroom, as I've learned from feedback gathered at various conferences.

Talking to teenage boys, it became clear that we're not always listening to the whole story. A group of Year 13 young men at one grammar school shared that while PSHE lessons aim to address masculinity, stereotypes and 'good behaviour,' they often feel outdated, lack clarity, and don't leave much room for students to learn from their mistakes.

We can mitigate some of these concerns by updating our curriculum content and lesson plans. Keeping up with current social and cultural issues is key to making lessons relevant to students' lives. Let's ensure diverse voices and experiences are represented – focusing on equitable representation of different genders, ethnicities, sexual orientations and socioeconomic backgrounds. Connecting PSHE lessons to real-world issues and current events makes learning more engaging. Sharing best practices and resources with colleagues can significantly reduce the burden on individual teachers. Prioritising student feedback and involving students in the curriculum development process can not only improve the quality of PSHE education but also reduce the teacher workload in the long run. During one visit to a school, I observed an effective approach where a small group of Sixth Form students engaged in a discussion about how our choice of language affects younger female students. The Sixth Formers asked the younger students to imagine using certain words and phrases when speaking to their mothers, sisters or female friends. The younger boys found it impactful to hear this feedback from 'older boys' within the school. This simple intervention encouraged young people to critically consider the impact of their language in different contexts.

Student voice is a powerful yet underutilised tool. Where possible, use older students who are willing to have these conversations with their peers. Student-led discussions can be highly influential, fostering empathy and understanding. Remember to provide guidance and support to students who are leading these discussions. (See also Chapter 13 on reverse mentoring and peer mentoring.)

One student aptly commented, 'It's difficult to listen to a teacher trying to tell us to steer clear of the likes of Tate, when they've only watched one of his videos, which we are told to stay away from.' This feedback underscores the need for more authentic and engaging approaches to teaching masculinity, allowing for deeper exploration and critical reflection.

TIP

Avoiding generic responses

Let's move beyond simplistic definitions and generic responses. Instead of one-size-fits-all lectures, consider:

- inviting male role models from diverse backgrounds to share their perspectives on masculinity
- encouraging open and honest discussions where students can share their own experiences and perspectives on gender roles and stereotypes
- connecting lessons with current events, news articles and social media content to illustrate the complexities of masculinity in contemporary society.

By challenging traditional notions of masculinity and encouraging students to critically examine their own beliefs and assumptions, we can help them to develop a more nuanced understanding of themselves and the world around them. Ultimately, the goal is to foster a classroom environment where open and honest conversations about gender, masculinity and equity can thrive. By empowering students to be active participants in their own learning, we can create a more inclusive and respectful school culture for all.

Whose story are you telling? Deficit narratives and diverse experiences

Many schools celebrate Pride Month, Black History Month or Disability Pride Month and are also actively auditing their curriculums to ensure students have a diverse and representative learning experience. But for too long, as Aisha Thomas aptly expressed in a workshop I attended, we have learned about diverse experiences through a 'deficit narrative'.

I discovered my own identity through the perspectives of colonialism, Empire, migration and being marginalised. My journey really began when I actively opted in to modules about diverse literature at university – and I loved every single lecture, seminar, book and essay. However, this realisation didn't occur until I was 19 years old.

The diversity we see in the classroom, particularly the 'well resourced' content for minoritised communities, frequently represents a deficit or limiting narrative.

Alan Turing is an oft-cited role model; however, as David Church highlights, Turing didn't necessarily have positive experiences. We also need to showcase LGBTQ+ role models who have had positive and empowering experiences too. Munroe Bergdorf is a brilliant example.

While she has faced trauma and adversity, her activism and work are inspiring for young people to learn about, particularly when considering belonging and inclusion from an intersectional point of view. You could:

- Discuss how she became the first transgender woman to front a L'Oréal campaign, highlighting her role in challenging beauty standards and increasing visibility for transgender individuals in the media.
- Explore her activism on issues such as racism, transphobia and social justice.
- Discuss her public statements on these issues and the impact they have had on public discourse.
- Read her book *Transitional*, which explores themes of identity, race and self-acceptance, or analyse her speeches and public appearances, focusing on her powerful and impactful communication style.

Students seeing themselves (or not) in the curriculum

Bilkis Miah, founder of the non-profit organisation You Be You, specialises in diversity and inclusion training and workshops for primary teachers and students. She told me that she learned very little about her Bangladeshi heritage until her twenties. 'You grow up in an environment where you are constantly seeking ways of fitting in with the dominant culture, with little time or space for you to fully embrace your cultural heritage,' she explains. This can lead many young people, particularly young people of colour, to experience a clash of cultures and be reminded of their differences, often unintentionally, as evidenced by my own school experience [see page 2].

The impact this has on a young person's sense of belonging in any environment, but especially at school, is profound and can have a lasting effect on their confidence, identity, and academic and career choices.

At the Diversifying the Curriculum Conference 2025, teacher Emily Folurunsho shared her thoughts on teaching Black British history effectively. She emphasised creating an inclusive classroom environment where all students feel able to participate in discussions. Using 19th-century migration to Britain as an example, she explained how teachers can explore the experiences of various communities, including Irish, Jewish and Eastern European groups, to demonstrate the complexity of cultural identity.

Folurunsho discussed how recent social movements have highlighted the need for more inclusive history teaching in schools. She explained that Black history is inherently part of British history and doesn't need to be treated as an additional topic. This approach, she noted, benefits all students – providing representation for Black students while helping others understand Britain's longstanding cultural diversity.

Going beyond recent immigration, she highlighted the presence of Black communities in Britain during medieval times and the Industrial Revolution. Folurunsho stressed the importance of teaching pre-colonial African history, noting that this broader context helps students understand how external forces shaped the continent's development and how racial concepts emerged from economic motivations.

We should carefully contextualise historical events: placing events like the Windrush generation within the broader context of mid-twentieth-century race relations in Britain. Centring Black voices is crucial, and utilising resources and perspectives from Black historians and scholars to ensure an authentic and accurate representation of Black British history.

Folurunsho emphasises the personal and cultural significance of learning about Black British history, sharing her own experiences as a Black Briton and the importance of seeing yourself reflected in the curriculum. The first time that students encounter a Black figure from history should not be through the lens of enslavement. For example, at Buckinghamshire New University, to celebrate the seventy-fifth anniversary of Windrush, Year 10 students from a local school were invited to participate in a Calypso music workshop with a Calypso artist, who not only taught students how to write a brilliant song, but also shared his experiences of Windrush and how values of hard work and joy in music shaped his livelihood (at the time he was working with refugee teenagers and using music as a form of therapy and support for their wellbeing).

We must proactively account for the disconnect in History teaching, asking *who* decides which histories are more important, and considering who is *remembered* and who this suggests *matters*. Folurunsho tells us that history has been distorted, disfigured and destroyed and that erased histories disempower people. She stresses the need to find untold stories and the stories of migration because these are empowering stories, hidden deep in our archives. It is a way of connecting the dots and answering the questions many minoritised students may have: how did we get here and why does it matter?

Krystian McInnis, the Co-Founder of Reimagining Education, reminds us to highlight the crucial distinction between diversifying the curriculum and truly decolonising it. He discusses the importance of acknowledging our own positionality, and recognising the power dynamics at play within the education system (see Chapter 3 for how to do this). Teachers need to redistribute power, centre the voices of marginalised communities, and challenge traditional Eurocentric perspectives on knowledge. This is a process of ongoing learning and unlearning, and of acknowledging that **decolonising the curriculum** requires continuous reflection and adjustment as an educator.

In acknowledging my own marginalised identity, I also recognise my privileges; it wasn't until I started teaching that I fully understood the experiences of disabled students, neurodivergent students and LGBTQ+ students. These students may be in a minority at your school; they may not see themselves represented in the curriculum, or if they do, they see themselves as the odd ones out. I did not grasp the feelings of parents and caregivers who send their children to mainstream schools, often unaware or uncertain of what their children might encounter in an environment where their identity is in the minority. Day by day as a teacher I realised how misunderstood and underestimated belonging in the classroom is.

Trauma-informed curriculum decisions

When I first heard the term 'trauma-informed practice', I'll admit I was dubious. It sounded like another initiative to add to our already full plates. But over time, I've seen how this approach transforms not just individual classrooms but entire school cultures – when it's done thoughtfully and systematically. Think of trauma-informed practice as a lens through which we view everything we do, from how we greet students in the morning to how we handle missed homework. It's not about adding new programmes or policies; it's about adapting our existing practices to better support all students, particularly those carrying invisible burdens.

The most successful schools I've worked with start small but think big. They might begin with simple changes – like rethinking the language we use around behaviour – while gradually building towards more comprehensive changes. This often means:

- Creating a shared understanding among staff about what trauma-informed practice actually looks like in our specific context. It's not enough to read about it; we need to discuss how it applies to our unique student population and school culture.
- Building capacity gradually through ongoing professional development – not just one-off training sessions that are quickly forgotten, but regular opportunities to reflect, discuss and adapt our practices.

Most importantly, they recognise that becoming trauma informed isn't a destination but a journey. It requires constant reflection and adjustment as we learn more about our students' needs and what works best in our context.

When we think about becoming trauma informed, it's helpful to understand it as a journey through distinct stages. The process begins with becoming trauma aware – this is when staff start recognising the signs and impact of trauma in their students, colleagues and the wider community. It's like developing a new lens through which to view behaviour and interactions.

Moving into the trauma-sensitive stage, schools begin to translate this awareness into understanding. It's not just about seeing trauma's effects, but realising that traditional approaches might need to change. During this stage, schools start building their knowledge base and examining how their systems and processes might need to adapt to better support both students and staff.

The trauma responsive stage marks a significant shift from understanding to action. This is when schools actively review and revise their policies and procedures to reflect trauma-informed principles. Rather than treating trauma awareness as an add-on, it becomes woven through all aspects of school life, as fundamental as equality and safeguarding policies.

Finally, becoming trauma informed means fully embedding these principles into daily school practice. But rather than seeing this as a final destination, trauma-informed schools recognise this as an ongoing journey of reflection and development. They're continuously learning, adapting their approaches based on experience and new understanding.

Trauma's impact on learning and behaviour

A **trauma-informed approach** isn't about diagnosing or treating trauma; it's about creating a classroom environment that is safe, supportive, and understanding of the potential impact of past experiences. Imagine your classroom as a sanctuary. It's essential to cultivate a safe space where students feel comfortable and secure. This means:

- **Creating a physical space:** designate a quiet corner or relaxation area where students can retreat when feeling overwhelmed.
- **Building emotional safety:** foster an open and honest environment where students feel comfortable sharing their feelings (if they choose to) without fear of judgment or criticism.
- **Establishing clear boundaries:** set and consistently uphold clear classroom rules and expectations to provide a sense of predictability and security.

Predictability and routine can be incredibly soothing for students who may have experienced trauma. Maintain a consistent daily routine to minimise uncertainty and anxiety. Clearly communicate expectations for behaviour and classroom participation. Consider co-creating these expectations with your students to foster a sense of ownership (see page 67 and the section on contracting). Use visual aids like schedules, timers and seating charts to help students to navigate the classroom environment.

It's also great for a teacher to model resilience and emotional wellbeing. If you're comfortable, share your own experiences with emotions, both positive and negative, to normalise emotional expression. Help students to understand how different situations can trigger different emotions, such as frustration, sadness or anger. Model healthy coping mechanisms, such as mindfulness exercises or deep breathing techniques.

In terms of curriculum considerations, you should carefully consider the potential impact of curricular topics on students. Some topics, such as violence, abuse or natural disasters, may trigger emotional responses. Inform students and parents in advance about sensitive topics that will be covered in class. This allows families to prepare their children as needed. Think about how you could offer alternative learning materials or activities for students who may find certain topics distressing.

Teachers should prioritise both growth and healing in their approach. This means taking time to acknowledge and validate students' experiences and feelings, while actively celebrating their successes – whether academic achievements or personal progress. By creating safe spaces where students can challenge themselves, they develop resilience. It's important to recognise every step forward, no matter how small it might seem, as part of their ongoing journey of growth.

Trauma-informed behaviour policies and processes

Let's look at your classroom practices through a trauma-informed lens. Start with language – the words we use matter deeply. Consider these shifts in how we frame things:

INSTEAD OF...	TRY...
'Punishment for disruption'	*'Support for regulation'*
'Breaking the rules'	*'Having a difficult moment'*
'Refusing to participate'	*'Finding participation challenging'*

Using words like 'punishment' and 'sanction' can inadvertently contribute to a punitive and potentially harmful environment for students who may have experienced trauma. These aren't just semantic changes. When we shift our language, we shift our thinking, and ultimately, our practice.

A student who's 'acting out' might actually be showing us they don't feel safe. By recognising this, we can respond with support rather than sanctions. Here's what this might look like in practice:

1. **Notice** A student repeatedly leaves their seat during quiet work time.
2. **Reframe** Instead of seeing this as 'disruptive behaviour', consider it might be a response to feeling overwhelmed.
3. **Respond** Create a quiet signal the student can use when they need a break.
4. **Support** Set up a designated calm space in your classroom which they can access when needed.

A truly trauma-informed approach to behaviour management recognises that challenging behaviours may stem from underlying trauma, such as abuse, neglect or exposure to violence. Instead of solely focusing on punishment, a trauma-informed approach emphasises understanding the root causes of these behaviours and providing support and interventions that address the underlying needs of the student.

Does the school's current behaviour policy consider the unique needs and experiences of all students?

- **Students in care** Have the policies been adapted to consider the specific needs and circumstances of children in foster care or other out-of-home placements? These students may face unique challenges, such as frequent transitions, attachment issues and exposure to trauma.

- **Refugee students** Have the policies considered the potential impact of trauma, displacement and cultural differences on the behaviour of refugee students?
- **Students from under-resourced households** Have the policies considered the impact of poverty, food insecurity and lack of resources on student behaviour and wellbeing?
- **Students with disabilities** Does the policy ensure that all students, including those with disabilities, have equal access to education and are supported in their learning and social-emotional development?

Behaviour policies and belonging are discussed on page 157, however, it is something to consider early on as you begin reading this book, to nurture a holistic culture of belonging in your school and classroom.

Building trauma-informed practices into our schools is an ongoing journey rather than a destination. While training sessions and CPD provide essential foundations, real change happens through daily practice, reflection and commitment from the whole school community. As we develop our understanding of trauma's impact on learning and behaviour, we strengthen our ability to create truly inclusive spaces where all students can feel safe, supported and ready to learn. Remember that this work takes time – both for staff development and cultural change – but each step towards becoming trauma informed has the potential to transform students' educational experiences and future outcomes.

12 Social Media

Gen Z,[26] Gen Alpha[27] and future generations will hardly know a world without an online presence. The 2023 Ofcom report, Teens on Screens, found that 51 per cent of teenagers 'thought they spent too much time on social media', which has increased by 10 per cent since 2021. A 2020 international study conducted by the think tank DQ Institute found that British children aged 8–19 spend an average of 44 hours a week looking at screens.[28] However, teenagers also report setting themselves more boundaries and wellbeing breaks.

While statistics provide a quantitative understanding of the scale of this issue, as teachers, we witness the impact of social media in our students first hand every day. While there can be positive aspects, the sheer volume of visual media and the accessibility of vast amounts of information, often unverified and unfiltered, pose significant challenges in the classroom.

One teacher aptly described this as a constant struggle to 'keep up' with the information and experiences their students are encountering before they even enter the classroom. Educators often find themselves navigating the unforeseen consequences of social media consumption without a clear understanding of the specific content or its impact on their students. This is on top of teaching a jam-packed curriculum too.

Perceived benefits and disadvantages of social media

In 2022, the Pew Research Center found that teens credit social media with strengthening their friendships, creativity and connection.[29] Thirty-two per cent of teenagers have said social media has a positive impact on them compared to only nine per cent saying it has had a negative effect. Sixty-seven per cent of teenagers have said social media platforms provide a sense of connection and community, especially when in need of support. There is an acknowledgement of the anxiety

---

[26]Born between the mid/late '90s and early 2010s.

[27]Born between the mid-2010s and early 2020s.

[28]www.telegraph.co.uk/politics/2020/02/10/british-children-spend-almost-two-days-week-screens-one-nation

[29]www.pewresearch.org/internet/2022/11/16/connection-creativity-and-drama-teen-life-on-social-media-in-2022

and overwhelm these platforms can cause, with 31 per cent saying social media can make them feel they have been left out of things by friends, 29 per cent feeling pressure to post popular content for the sake of 'likes and comments' and 23 per cent saying the platforms make them feel worse about their own lives. Yet, the overarching 'teen voice' in the Pew research still suggests a positive outlook on social media.

This may be problematic (and confusing) for teachers and parents, who may see the positives of social media but are well aware of the negative impact it seems to have on younger generations.

In his book *The Anxious Generation: How the Great Rewiring of Childhood is Causing an Epidemic of Mental Illness*, Johnathan Haidt draws a compelling connection between the alarming rise in anxiety, depression and self-harm observed across Western nations and the escalating accessibility of technology. Haidt explains this partly through the decline of free (outdoor) play during childhood, which he puts down to the perception that the world has become less safe. Hand in hand with this, Haidt argues, is the rise of what he calls the 'phone-based childhood', which started in the late 2000s and accelerated with the rise of smartphones (containing internet access and social media apps).

I spoke to an ex-student about this on my podcast, *School Should Be....* I connected with Simranjeet, after I learned she launched a successful YouTube channel to help students interested in a career in law, aiming to make the experience of applying for careers in law more accessible and equitable. In the podcast episode I recorded with her, I asked her how she managed some of the problematic situations caused by social media that impact teen wellbeing and health. Simranjeet, who attended school between 2007 and 2010, observed that while social media was present during her formative years (Years 7–9), its impact was significantly less pervasive than it is today. Social media was spoken about at school, but didn't exert as much influence as it does for young people now, enabling Simranjeet and her peers to maintain healthier boundaries and friendships within the school environment. This observation is corroborated by findings from Ofcom's 'Children's Media Lives' study, which has been conducted for a decade. The study reveals a shift in online behaviour: highlighting a decline in social interaction and creative expression. Instead, it emphasises the dominance of 'fast-paced and short-form' content consumption, pervasive social pressure, and an increasing focus on carefully curating an online persona.

Numerous long-term studies have unequivocally demonstrated the detrimental effects of smartphones on sleep quality and duration. These sleep disruptions have been directly linked to a range of mental health challenges, including depression, anxiety and increased irritability. Moreover, sleep deprivation significantly impacts cognitive function, leading to impaired learning and lower academic performance.

Since our phones are constantly interrupting us, our ability to focus is severely impaired. I'm sure you've noticed it in yourself, as well as your students. (I often scroll on my phone while watching TV – it's called 'second screening' and is very common.) Every ping, buzz and chime demands our attention, pulling us away from whatever task we're engaged in. These frequent interruptions fragment our thought processes and make it difficult to maintain a sustained focus.

While we may think we're multitasking by checking our phones while working, studies have shown that true multitasking is an illusion. Our brains are actually rapidly switching between tasks, leading to decreased efficiency and increased errors. The allure of social media, games and other apps can easily lead us to procrastinate, and all of this constant connectivity definitely contributes to feelings of anxiety and stress. The fear of missing out (FOMO) and the pressure to constantly be 'on' makes it difficult to relax and truly disconnect.

Finally, our tweens and teens are getting a huge dopamine hit (what's known as 'the happy hormone') each time they use their phone. Just like other addictions, they keep going back to things that make them feel good, like scrolling through social media or playing games. Companies design their tech, apps and games precisely to be habit forming. But, over time, our brains get used to these interactions, so we need more and more of these things to get that same level of dopamine high. This is called neuroadaptation, and it can lead to serious problems.

All of this is, rightly, very worrying and might make us teachers feel a bit lost. What can we possibly do to combat this huge issue? One idea is to remove phones from the equation altogether. Several schools have now implemented a mobile phone ban. Nearly three-quarters of primary schools collect phones at the start of the school day. In secondary schools, rules have become stricter too, with 60 per cent of students unable to use their phones under any circumstance during the school day.[30] Your classroom (and other areas such as the library or dining hall) could be phone-free zones. Consider introducing secure lockers for students to store their phones during school hours. If this seems unlikely, think about ways you can integrate more hands-on activities like experiments, art projects and group work into your teaching, minimising the need for technology.

To effectively implement phone rules, involving students in the process is crucial. By facilitating class discussions, brainstorming rules together and reaching a consensus, students feel ownership over the guidelines. Clear and consistent communication of the rules, visual cues and fair enforcement are essential. Emphasising the benefits of reduced phone use (such as improved focus, enhanced social interaction and increased engagement) and responsible phone use, including lessons about misinformation

[30](31/01/2023) Strike update, phone rules and restorative justice! – teacher Tapp. Available at: https://teachertapp.co.uk/articles/strike-update-phone-rules-and-restorative-justice (Accessed: 03 January 2025).

and disinformation, may help students to use their phones responsibly to enhance their own wellbeing and health.

Schools should also actively engage with parents and carers to address this issue. This includes hosting workshops for parents on responsible technology use and the importance of screen time limits (record them for parents with demanding schedules). Open communication between teachers, parents and students about technology's challenges (and benefits) is crucial for creating a shared understanding and supportive environment.

The impact of online information-sharing

In many ways, social media and scrolling have become another form of learning for today's young people. Students constantly absorb information, opinions and perspectives through social media feeds. This is a form of informal learning, even if it's not structured or intentional. Social media shapes students' understanding of the world, values and social interactions. It influences their knowledge base in ways that educators may not fully understand or be able to control. And, perhaps they shouldn't, given the rise of AI and how learning is constantly evolving beyond the classroom and books we teach.

I am very aware that teachers are under a great deal of pressure, and with free information distributed at a rate none of us can keep up with, it is nearly impossible to address all of the harmful and dangerous content our young people are exposed to.

Finding time in classroom discussions to talk about the different media students consume, and how to consume it, can help control what can seem like an uncontrollable online world. It is by no means a fixed or holistic solution. Navigating it will need to become a constant in schools, just like deciphering Shakespeare (enter subjects such as Computer Science and topics like digital literacy). Speaking to teachers, I have sensed (and experienced) their exasperation, particularly when, as a teacher, 'in real life' you are trying to resolve the harmful effects of misinformation and disinformation, online bullying, students feeling isolated and consumed by 'follows', 'likes' and being 'blocked'.

Unfortunately, the rise of social media and the speed at which information is gathered and shared (a blessing and a curse), can mean we have lost or are losing a culture of forgiveness. One problem is that it can make people afraid to talk openly because they worry about their words being shared publicly and taken out of context. This can stop students from learning and growing because they're afraid to make mistakes. We need to create a classroom where students feel safe to try new things, share their ideas and learn from their mistakes.

TIP

Encourage students to think about their online persona and digital footprints. Social media pressure defines who to be, what to want, how to look, and what or what not to say. Social comparison is rife, as are peer interactions that can support or disapprove of our identities. Nurturing psychologically safe cultures in the classroom can help alleviate these issues.

Some phrases I've found helpful:

- *'Before you post something online, ask yourself: Does this truly reflect who I am? Am I comfortable with how I'm presenting myself?'*
- *'Use your phone to take pictures and videos of things you want to remember. But don't just look at the screen! Try to enjoy the moment and experience it for yourself.'*
- *'Remember it's OK not to post everything. You can keep some parts of your life private or just for offline.'*

Toxic masculinity and online misogyny

Toxic masculinity refers to harmful behaviours and attitudes associated with traditional gender roles for men, such as aggression, dominance and emotional suppression. Andrew Tate[31] is an internet personality known for promoting these harmful ideals, often through misogynistic and violent rhetoric. Toxic masculinity affects both boys and girls, limiting boys' emotional expression and perpetuating harmful stereotypes about women. In the classroom, it can manifest as bullying, disrespect, and limited career aspirations for both genders.

The rise of figures like Andrew Tate highlights the complex challenges presented by social media. A female student commented, 'I don't like him, but he's very entertaining.' While some students may recognise the harmful nature of his rhetoric, the 'entertainment factor' he provides can be difficult to resist, as illustrated by this observation. This underscores how social media can inadvertently normalise and even glamorise harmful ideologies, particularly those that perpetuate toxic masculinity.

As a millennial, I realised that the amount of time Generation Z and Generation Alpha spend with one another 'in real life' is sadly decreasing. I tried to put myself in the shoes of the young people talking to me and I empathised, thinking back to my own experience going to a single-sex school: upon leaving, I worried about socialising

[31]Andrew Tate is merely a better-known example of toxic masculinity; other examples include Jordan Peterson, Gavin McInnes, Milo Yiannopoulos and Roosh V.

with boys, and that was without the wider pressures of social media. When speaking to students at an all-boys school, it was somewhat nostalgic and humbling to learn that, in 2023, they felt the same. For young boys to confidently navigate their 'way out' of negative online influences, we must intentionally talk about lessons and topics they are interested in.

TIP

Below are some ideas, which can be incorporated into the PSHE curriculum, where there is time to address these issues:

- **Go beyond basic 'fake news' identification**
    - *Analyse popular, gendered and stereotyped memes and videos together in class. Discuss their underlying messages, logical fallacies and emotional appeals.*
    - Explore the concept of 'echo chambers' and how algorithms can isolate users within extremist online communities.
    - *Use tools like Media Bias/Fact Check to analyse the credibility of different news sources and online content.*
- **Deconstruct the 'red pill' philosophy**
    - *Openly discuss the 'red pill' metaphor and its origins.*
    - Analyse how it's used to promote misogynistic and harmful ideologies.
    - *Encourage students to question the assumptions and biases underlying these beliefs.*
- **Challenge masculinities**
    - Introduce diverse male role models: discuss athletes, artists and activists who challenge traditional stereotypes of masculinity. Explore characters in literature and film who exhibit qualities like empathy, vulnerability and emotional intelligence.
    - Promote healthy emotional expression: encourage open and honest discussions about emotions, including vulnerability and sadness. Challenge the stigma around seeking help for mental health issues. Provide resources for boys to develop healthy coping mechanisms for stress and frustration.
    - *Redefine 'success': discuss the limitations of traditional definitions of success (e.g. wealth, power, dominance). Emphasise the importance of personal growth, meaningful relationships and contributing to society.*

'Toxic masculinity'? Or intersectional masculinity?

When I first proposed this chapter, I called it 'overcoming toxic masculinity'. However, over the past couple of years, I've realised just how damaging that phrase can be for boys, girls, non-binary students and those of us wanting to nurture safe and inclusive classrooms for every student. How do we create safe spaces without cisgendered boys feeling vulnerable or targeted by stereotypes? While I understand that we, as educators and experts in these areas, can critically understand the word 'toxic', a young teenager may not view the word 'toxic' in a critical and evaluative manner. Instead, they may feel attacked, ashamed, angry and misunderstood. We need to facilitate lessons, conversations and environments that help young people to navigate masculinity, femininity and individuality in a cohesive, inclusive, joyful and nurturing way.

On balance, I encourage staff and students to steer away from using the term 'toxic masculinity'. Looking back on blogs and pieces I have published and been involved in, I would also revise my use of the term, too. I say this because the word 'toxic' means unpleasant, poisonous or something that causes harm. When paired with masculinity, it can imply that masculinity is inherently 'bad', which is not true. Ultimately, I've come to feel that the term 'toxic masculinity' is unhelpful in the classroom because it can presuppose that 'male' behaviour is toxic from the outset.

Exploring masculinity in other subjects

TIP

When looking for ways to integrate belonging and inclusion into your classroom, don't reinvent the wheel! Look for existing opportunities within your current curriculum and schemes of work. Conduct a curriculum and scheme of work audit with your department and colleagues. Add questions that address belonging, inclusion, respect and dignity to your lesson plans. This approach seamlessly integrates these crucial elements into the existing teaching and learning process, rather than treating diversity and inclusion as an 'add-on'.

I found teaching *Romeo and Juliet* a fantastic example of how to explore masculinity and toxic behaviours, within the existing curriculum. Consider this line:

> *'O sweet Juliet,/Thy beauty hath made me effeminate /And in my temper soften'd valour's steel!' (3.1.114-116)*

This quote, spoken by Romeo, sparks powerful discussions about masculinity, femininity, and toxic behaviours.

- Is it Romeo's relationship with Juliet that has 'weakened' him, or is it the careless actions and fight between Tybalt and Mercutio?
- What choices and situations have led to the tragedy?
- Is it as simple as labelling this 'toxic masculinity', or is there an *absence* of something else such as vulnerability, humility, honesty and open communication)?

Subjects like English naturally lend themselves to these challenging conversations about inclusion and belonging but we can integrate them into other subject lessons, too. It can be incredibly helpful for classroom teachers to intentionally consider how concepts of masculinity might relate to their specific subject matter. Where might there be opportunities to weave into lessons discussions about positive psychology, healthy friendships and respectful relationships? Where might elements of 'toxic' masculinity arise within the curriculum itself?

Some suggestions for other subjects:

- **English** Explore traditional masculine traits and stereotypes. Discuss the complexities of romantic and platonic love, including healthy flirting and courting practices. Engage in discussions about vulnerability and masculinity.
- **Science** Explore stereotypes associated with male strength. Discuss the impact of hormonal changes on students, both physically and emotionally. Examine the effects of emotional regulation and body image.
- **History and Economics** Discuss patriarchy, the gender pay gap, and how societal and economic gender roles continue to impact young people today.
- **Geography** Explore how gender influences urbanisation and tourism. Analyse the impact of stereotypes and gender roles on crime rates and success in different countries.
- **Music** Analyse song lyrics and their influence on perceptions of masculinity and gender roles.
- **Mathematics** Observe classroom dynamics. Who raises their hand to answer questions? What are the interactions like between students of different genders?

This goes beyond thematic units and encourages a broader consideration of gender equity within STEM subjects.

'Toxic masculinity' is the subject of this section, but it's important to remember that it's not the central focus of most lessons or your everyday classroom. This is true for all the topics we explore in this book. However, these issues and the conversations they spark are inherently woven into the fabric of our classrooms. As educators, we work with people and the impact of these conversations, on our students, our classrooms and our own practice, can be profound.

So, we must gain confidence in creating opportunities to naturally weave these conversations into our lessons. The more we do this, the less daunting they become. We must encourage young people to engage in honest and open discussions within a trusting and safe environment.

Schooling accounts for approximately 20 per cent of an individual's life (considering the average life expectancy and the fact that most students stay in education until 18). Also, these years are usually our most formative and impact our values, thoughts, triggers and traumas (which is why social media and the media generally have a lasting influence on us at this age). Students spend so much time with you as teachers, so we have a real opportunity to nurture a safe and inclusive learning environment where students can have difficult conversations, particularly male students for whom we know having conversations and being vulnerable does not always come easy. We see this in school every day as boys struggle to talk about their mental and emotional health due to gender stereotypes.

As educators, we need to consider the diverse experiences and challenges facing our students, particularly when it comes to gender dynamics and relationships. In a recent blog post[32] exploring student voices, I reflected on whether we're truly listening to all our students' experiences: the boy who sees strong female role models at home, the students processing racial trauma, Muslim boys navigating complex identity issues, or those struggling with traditional expectations of masculinity. We need to hear from students who don't fit conventional patterns – whether that's boys who avoid sports, young people exploring their sexuality, or those carrying heavy family responsibilities. Just as importantly, we should acknowledge positive experiences too: the girls with supportive male family members, and the students of all genders who model healthy, respectful relationships. These voices challenge simplistic narratives and remind us of the complex reality of gender dynamics in our schools.

As well as role models, there are several ways in which we can embed LGBTQ+ awareness into the curriculum, particularly in subjects like Religious Education, Law and Science. Students can explore:

---

[32]What if we replace toxic masculinity with intersectional masculinity? | Diverse Educators

- Section 28 and its legacy on society and the law.
- LGBTQ+ communities and faith (a difficult and sensitive discussion point but, with the use of contracting and clear and boundaried discussion etiquette, you can explore the topic so students can see how diverse and intersectional our communities are). However, this can be a rather traumatic and challenging discussion. The charity, Just Like Us, have some fantastic speakers that can share their nuanced lived experiences about faith and being a part of the LGBTQ+ community. If you have local faith and interfaith leaders in your school community and network, it is worth getting in touch with them to help facilitate this discussion.
- In Science, students can discuss sex and gender in a safe and secure environment.

These discussions can also be tricky with the wider school community, with parents, carers and families in particular. Many families and individuals will challenge these discussions taking place in school. It can help to approach all responses to these topics with compassion: everyone is trying to keep their own children safe and everyone wants to ensure their personal values are not compromised. While a daunting task, we can, over time, reassure parents and families that neither need be compromised:

- Ensure that families, carers and stakeholders understand your school's mission statement, values and inclusive school culture, that is, to ensure every student belongs, feels safe and is a valued member of the school. You may emphasise this at open evenings, on your website, in your school contract with parents and in regular communications with the school community, such as a termly newsletter.
- Be transparent about the aims of challenging and diverse discussions at school: they are impartial, they promote understanding, empathy and compassion for all students, they are important so that every student is seen, heard and valued. The challenging and diverse conversations are not to convince, persuade or encourage students about what is 'right' and what is 'wrong', rather the opposite. The aims of the discussions are to create a culture of belonging so that students have the opportunity to share, listen and learn about different lived experiences, thoughts and feelings so that they develop into responsible global citizens.
- Remind families that you, as teachers, are qualified and highly trained professionals that use social and cultural awareness to ensure all discussions are navigated ethically, responsibly and safely. You are impartial and the discussions and knowledge shared about sensitive topics are managed safely and sensibly, appropriate to different age groups.

- Remind families that discrimination, bullying and harassment are a sad reality for so many students, particularly students who are minoritised and feel underrepresented and misrepresented at school and in the media. Every family, parent and carer wants their child to feel safe and these discussions are an opportunity to help overcome and mitigate bullying and harassment.
- Give families an opportunity to share their thoughts, questions and concerns with you. It can help to do this initially via a questionnaire using Google Form. This can lead into a 'talk shop' where families are invited into school to talk about what their children are learning and experiencing at school. It can help to have representatives from different communities present at these sessions, *if* they feel comfortable to be there – while people have their concerns, we cannot put the emotional and physical safety of vulnerable communities at risk.
- It is important to let parents know explicitly that any discussion (whether it is about faith, LGBTQ+, global warming or a Shakespearean play!) can be challenging and lead to students expressing strong opinions. However, continue to reiterate your professionalism and expertise in managing these discussions.

While this can seem daunting for us as teachers, it is important to be kind to yourself and know that you are not expected to have all the answers. Equally, this yet again emphasises why the overarching school mission, values and CPD are so important: school leaders should prioritise specialist training and development for staff if school staff are to feel confident and able to navigate nuanced and inclusive discussions. If we build these discussions into the curriculum, there will be effective planning and development time, so you can feel more confident conducting these discussions. You should also revisit the idea of contracting and the phrase banks to support these discussions, too (see page 67 in Chapter 6).

A lack of male role models?

One of the dominant narratives, particularly on social media, is that young people lack positive male role models. I agreed with this for a while and have written about it. However, after speaking with young people and spending a bit of time on YouTube and social media, there doesn't seem to be a lack of male role models, but there are different perceptions about what makes a positive role model for young male students. As teachers, we can aim to teach students about what makes a positive role model.

In a social media, internet and algorithm-driven world, one definition of a role model is their popularity and visual success online. YouTube, Instagram and TikTok are governed by algorithmic popularity (likes, impressions, views and follows). There are plenty of men, with millions of likes, for young people to 'follow' and be influenced by. We cannot underestimate the extent to which social media has rewired young people's perceptions of role models and success.

However, there *is* a lack of men in the public eye talking about the things young men need to know about, such as healthy relationships (romantic and platonic), body image and mental health. Alex, who was in Year 13 when interviewed and is now reading medicine at university, believes we need to present young men with 'desirable' and relatable male role models offline.

Andrew Tate, a former kickboxer who was arrested as part of an investigation into human trafficking, rape and organised crime, has a public persona as an influencer and internet personality. For many young people, he is considered a role model as what he represents (the fame, fortune, success, his knowledge and advice) is what many young people aspire to. Part of the problem with Tate dominating the male landscape of social media is that toxic masculinity is now defined as sexist and misogynistic behaviours when, in reality, it is much more than that.

Toxic masculinity is toxic because of many other social and economic pressures placed on young men: boys should (supposedly) be aesthetically 'fit', tall, good at sports, funny, strong, high achievers, chivalrous and 'the provider'. As a teacher, it is not my 'job' to tell students if this is right or wrong. However, as a teacher who cares about student wellbeing and is concerned about the rise in poor mental health and wellbeing of boys (and obviously girls and all teenage students), it is important to understand and recognise the pressures students in my classroom are under.

Understanding masculinity requires acknowledging the diverse cultural contexts students bring to the classroom. Some students may have grown up seeing certain masculine traits as positive or desirable, shaped by their family experiences and societal influences. As a teacher, your role is to create a space for exploration rather than judgement. Invite students to reflect critically by asking open-ended questions: How do different representations of masculinity affect you personally? What impact do you see on your friends, peers and in social media? By framing the discussion around lived experiences and personal insights, you can guide students towards understanding and empathy, moving beyond simplistic 'right' or 'wrong' narratives.

However, while we can do this *in* our classrooms, one glance outside the classroom and school playground reminds us of the social and economic pressures that surround boys and men. Online influencers who are wealthy, successful, popular and strong are glamorised, celebrated and portrayed as desirable. They're not always wrong either: some of their messaging is balanced and sensible – why wouldn't we want young men to work hard, take care of their health and believe in themselves? Aren't these some of the messages we try to convey in school anyway? In a classroom where we say that debate and diverse opinions are celebrated, freedom of speech is welcome and if we want to empower young people with a voice, we need to be prepared with clear reasons and explanations why students should be mindful about admiring the likes of Tate. A few male students have also told me that while discussion about the **manosphere** and alpha males is constantly shut down by teachers and adults, they aren't offered any alternatives either.

Positive role modelling

We are constantly searching for people to role model positive behaviours, which is good practice. However, in reality it's is not always possible, given the time constraints and pressures put on schools. Along with our teenagers, who effectively live online, teachers and carers live in a busy world too and even with the best of intentions, it isn't easy to reconfigure social media algorithms that feel beyond our control. Instead of looking to replace social media role models and the control it has over our young people, we can create classroom and school environments that encourage critical thinking, curiosity and discussion to challenge and question the notion of 'toxic masculinity' taking over the lives of young people.

If we want young men to steer away from troubling content and to be able to navigate it sensibly and safely, we need to talk to them about the content they are surrounded by. To do this, provide a space for young men to talk about it. Who do they admire? Why? Who do they follow? Why? We need to listen to them before we judge or critique them. This may be in PSHE lessons, form time, or during a lunchtime or after-school club about inclusion or wellbeing for young men.

ACTIVITY

Ask staff and students about their role models. Why have they chosen that person? Role models don't have to be famous or in the media spotlight – it's important to highlight the lived experiences of people our students can relate to. Engaging the school community can be extremely uplifting and empowering.

Social media and polarisation

Social media, in many ways, is designed to tap into our raw emotions. It feels angry or extremely happy; the algorithms favour love or hate – there isn't much room for nuance or balance. These attitudes can permeate the classroom, especially if, as the reports above suggest, teenagers are more likely to be consuming content than discussing what they see.

Many boys who become involved in the 'manosphere' aren't initially driven by hate. They may be seeking support and community online, feeling lost or isolated. However, social media algorithms amplify extreme content, gradually exposing users to more and more radical ideas. This can be a slippery slope. When boys feel rejected by their peers and society at large, they can be drawn to groups that offer a sense of belonging and validation. The manosphere provides this, but at a significant cost. By embracing these extreme ideologies, men risk becoming further isolated and radicalised, ultimately embracing harmful and hateful views. Radicalisation often involves introducing newcomers to radical ideas, sometimes using terms like 'red pilling' and 'black pilling'. These groups target men in online spaces like bodybuilding forums or gaming communities, seeking to attract and groom new followers.

A few young people told me that they don't really know *how* to talk about the things they see online. Some also said they didn't *think* to bring them up either. I found the latter interesting. I am no psychologist, but while young people are spending time consuming information online, perhaps they are just taking in what they see without always questioning or discussing it. Equally, some do bring it up, but out of context – in the middle of a lesson, with parents and carers, amongst peers who may not be consuming the same content – or in environments where they do not feel safe or comfortable.

I still remember a time, several years ago now, when a couple of my students started telling me about the 'dark web'. It was a brief conversation, which came up during a lesson with a class I had a great relationship with. They were amused by my naivety (I was genuinely shocked), but equally, I used my position as their teacher to tell them how to stay safe online and to talk to me, a trusted adult, if they see something or come across anything they want to talk about. While I was (and still am) unable to control what they see and access online, I can let them know that the classroom and school is a place where they can feel safe, have trusting conversations and, importantly, seek support should they need it. I asked them if their parents knew and they all laughed and said no. While a minor conversation in the classroom, it provided a lens into the world of young people: we cannot assume that just because we are their care givers (parents, families and teachers), they will feel comfortable sharing their thoughts and feelings with us. Hence, building trusting relationships and environments that enable discussion are so important and a great opportunity in the classroom. These experiences were not unique to me as a teacher and I am sure there are many teachers who have had similar, important, but 'off topic' discussions in their lessons too. This is one of many examples of micro, brief interactions in the classroom that can make all the difference to a student's feeling of belonging and safety at school.

Social media and news consumption

What does it mean for our teaching when six in ten of our students get their news from social media? According to Ofcom's 2022 report, while teenagers increasingly turn to social platforms for information, they're also sceptical about what they find there. Most still trust their families (68 per cent) and television (65 per cent) more than social media for reliable news.[33] This creates an opportunity for us as teachers – we can help students to develop critical thinking skills by using their natural scepticism as a starting point for media literacy discussions, comparing how different sources cover the same story and creating classroom activities that help students to evaluate online information.

How to help students with social media literacy

Teachers increasingly bear the responsibility of instructing students on the validity and reliability of information sources. But, let's be realistic: teaching digital literacy can feel overwhelming when we're already juggling so many priorities. However, we can weave it naturally into our existing lessons without creating extra work. For instance, when starting a new topic, take a few minutes to ask students to compare the first three Google results they find. What's different about each source? Who wrote them? These quick conversations normalise critical thinking about online information.

Similarly, those moments when you notice phones appearing under desks can become impromptu learning opportunities. Instead of just asking students to put them away, use it as a springboard to discuss how social media algorithms shape what they see. When covering current events, pull up different news sources and explore how each tells the story differently. These discussions don't need to derail your lesson – even five minutes can plant important seeds of critical thinking.

You don't need to reinvent the wheel here. Organisations like the News Literacy Project offer ready-to-use lesson plans, while AllSides Media helps students to understand multiple perspectives on current events. Common Sense Media also provides excellent age-appropriate resources for digital citizenship. These tools can help you to feel more confident addressing digital literacy without becoming a social media expert yourself.

The goal isn't to transform our students into professional fact-checkers. Rather, we want them to develop the habit of questioning what they see online. Sometimes, all it takes is one thoughtful question – *'How do we know this is true?'* – to spark valuable

[33] www.ofcom.org.uk/media-use-and-attitudes/media-habits-children/children-and-parents-media-use-and-attitudes-report-2022/ – April 2024

discussions about information literacy. These small moments, integrated naturally into our teaching, can have a lasting impact on how students navigate their digital world.

Teach students about misinformation and disinformation

Misinformation is inaccurate and false information. Disinformation is false information which is *intentionally* shared to spread lies, fear and scepticism. Both are similar and can cause harm; however, disinformation will *purposefully* set out to cause harm. Both can have a negative effect on a student's and teacher's sense of belonging and safety in the classroom and, therefore, it is very important to teach students how to be critical of the information they can freely access.

Build activities and lessons to help students identify and talk about misinformation and disinformation. These activities and lessons may seem more appropriate for subjects like English, History, PSHE, Psychology, Geography, and so on, but, every teacher can begin with the definitions of both terms and find examples of each within their subject area to explore with students. For example:

- In Maths, you could explore 'mathematical myths' with Key Stage 3 classes as an engaging way to discuss the impact of misinformation and disinformation. It could be something as simple as *'Using a calculator means you're no good at Maths',* or something a little more controversial such as, *'Boys are better at Maths than girls, which is why more boys do Maths at A level and go into jobs like engineering and accounting.'* Displaying statements like these on the board can spark interesting discussions and encourage students to discuss the impact of this type of information.
- For Key Stage 5 Physical Education students, you may choose something a little more challenging, such as a discussion about Imane Khelif and the mis- and disinformation that went viral during the summer of 2024. A critical point to raise here is the level of verified sources online that were also spreading misinformation about the Olympian. At Key Stage 4, you can address the race riots of 2024, caused by the tragic murders of three young children in Southport. This topic is particularly relevant to English, Media Studies, Psychology and PSHE. Teachers can begin by communicating that all students in their classroom are safe and respected, and that the lesson or discussion is to help students navigate some of the content they may have seen online and on the news. In English and Media Studies, this may involve teaching the definitions of misinformation and disinformation and analysing headlines and media sources, including visual media and social media posts. In Psychology, this may include exploring the impact on communities and the importance of trauma-informed support.

- Encourage authenticity in real life and online. If you feel comfortable, you could model this by sharing personal stories or insights to encourage students to be more open. Try to help students avoid the pressure to create an idealised online persona by encouraging self-acceptance (maybe through constructive feedback, peer encouragement or self-reflection activities).
- As with real-life debate, talk to students about the importance of checking in with themselves – before liking, commenting, or sharing content, they could pause and consider the impact of those actions.

As teachers, particularly secondary subject specialists, you will be in the best position to know how to approach certain topics through your subject matter. These discussions, particularly the final two bullet points, are challenging, and as teachers read this, I wholly understand the desire to stay away from these topics and to proceed with caution. Instead, frame the discussion and clarify the intention – real examples will be used to discuss an objective of the lesson: to understand the impact of misinformation and disinformation.

In-person communication skills

Debates and discussions, especially for the post-COVID generation, are necessary to create classrooms where students feel safe and can share their opinions and thoughts. Many current secondary-aged students have spent important years listening, observing – with minimal conversation – through a screen. Of course, there is a very valid argument that we cannot just blanket ban digital media, or the technology used to access the online world, especially as students need to be digitally literate for the future world of work they will inhabit.

There are so many benefits to online and remote learning. However, we have a generation of teenagers who predominantly use screens and tech to communicate. While we don't yet know what the future holds, students in our classrooms today are working with millennials and Gen X; they are also working with fellow students with different levels of access to technology and the digital world.

The online space does not wholly provide a real-life space to communicate in person and read body language and social cues, such as eye contact, hesitations and facial expressions, which can be just as valuable as verbal language. This is so important for the world of work, interviews and presentations, as well as for having one-to-one conversations, challenging and brave conversations, resolving conflicts, friendships, relationships, and more. The latter are fundamental social skills.

Going back to *The Anxious Generation*, Haidt puts forward the theory that real-life (successful) forms of communication rely on body language. They also happen in sync with others, generally occur in sequence and with a few individuals at a time. Online activity has clearly completely disrupted this rhythm.

I spoke to a group of Sixth Formers about this. When asked about conflict, miscommunication and general barriers they experience in relationships, they all said there are fewer and fewer opportunities to socialise in person – and they all wanted more. The classroom is one of the few places left where they can have 'real-life' discussions, conversations, disagreements and a laugh with one another that doesn't include an emoji (although, as a millennial, I do love an emoji!). The more I talk to young people, parents and teachers, it's clear that feelings of loneliness in schools and classrooms have been exacerbated by social media. Teachers can foster a sense of community by organising social events, encouraging participation in school activities, and promoting offline activities like sports, reading and spending time in nature. These initiatives provide opportunities for face-to-face interaction, fostering a sense of belonging and helping students to develop strong social connections.

TIP

Encourage face-to-face communication and social interaction through debates, presentations and peer tutoring.

The impact of social media on the student–teacher relationship experience as a teacher, alongside reports such as Ofcom's referenced earlier, have shown me that school-aged children are now more likely to seek answers online and outside of the classroom than ever before. (Although parents, home and community have a major influence on young people, we cannot underestimate the impact of social media news on young people either.) While there are many pros to the level of free knowledge, particularly the diversity of knowledge available online, it seems that levels of 'connectedness' online (or simply being so connected to our phones and social media applications) have also led to a disconnect between students and their teachers.

Students increasingly rely on online sources for information, often bypassing traditional classroom learning. This can lead to a situation where students possess a wealth of knowledge about a topic, often gleaned from fragmented online sources, while teachers may not be as readily familiar with the specific details or nuanced opinions circulating on social media. This can create a knowledge gap and hinder effective classroom discussions. The constant stream of information and opinions on social media can overwhelm students and make it difficult for them to process and synthesise information effectively. This can manifest in classroom settings as a lack of focus, difficulty engaging in in-depth discussions, and a reliance on quick, easily accessible online answers rather than critical thinking and deeper analysis.

This is something I have spoken at length about to teachers. Some teachers find they intentionally have to keep up to date with current events on social media – and not just the event itself but for the tens of hundreds of opinions and comments that follow. For teachers and schools, this can create an extra layer or barrier to establishing belonging and inclusion in the classroom. For secondary schools, this can feel very challenging, as these are the years students develop a sense of self, identity, curiosity and more. Some teachers and staff do not have social media accounts, or engage in it minimally (and they are absolutely entitled to do this). Perhaps for the first time in the history of mainstream education, there seems to be a great 'connection gap' between students and their teachers, which can feel quite dangerous and vulnerable. While processing a ton of information, the skills or outlets for discussing and talking about what they consume are minimal. If we add the general pressures of everyday schooling to this, school and the classroom can feel lonely for young people if they cannot connect or talk to the adults in the room.

Ultimately, this 'connection gap' threatens to undermine the very foundation of education: meaningful human interaction. While the digital world offers unprecedented access to information, it can also isolate students and create a barrier between them and their teachers. By fostering open and honest dialogue about the impact of social media, and by prioritising real-life connections and authentic classroom experiences, we can bridge this gap and ensure that our students feel supported, understood and connected to their learning community.

Time for tech?

Of course, the ideal solution would be to integrate lessons on digital literacy, responsible online behaviour, and the critical evaluation of information into our day-to-day teaching. But contrary to popular belief, unless teacher training, the curriculum and school dynamics are to change drastically, teachers can't focus that heavily on social media literacy as well as their subject area and increasing curriculum demands, particularly as students progress through to Key Stages 4 and 5. It is covered in subjects like PSHE, and many curriculum areas integrate social media modules. But relative to the level of exposure and speed at which AI and social media is developing, it is near impossible for teachers to keep up. The educational system has yet to consistently and comprehensively define and teach online kindness, respect and civility. However, some resources are available, such as the Common-Sense Media guides, which can inform conversations around many key aspects of digital citizenship.

TIP

By emphasising within the classroom that our words have consequences, even when expressed behind a screen, we can help children to grasp the importance of online courtesy and respect, mirroring their significance in real-life interactions.

Responding to social media issues

One of the most difficult experiences in the classroom is when you feel like you have lost control; it breeds feelings of uncertainty, which can feel very uncomfortable in a classroom full of teenagers. Therefore, it is easier to be the first one to confront and address topics students will have seen and heard about on social media. Some teachers have said to me they do not want to keep 'on top of' social media trends and news, as it can become all-consuming for them too. But you don't need to. The likelihood is, you have an inkling that something may be affecting a student's sense of belonging and safety in the classroom, particularly minoritised students. There may be other teachers and students who comment on it in your classroom and in the staffroom. It may be gut instinct telling you to address what you are sensing and reinforce inclusion for everyone.

If you are unsure about the topic, there is merit in telling the class:

> *'I can see this is something worthy of discussion and we will address it in another lesson this week. I need to go away and do my own reading and understanding and some fact-checking. How about we all go and look at different sources and come back in a couple of days for a conversation about it?'*

This approach of acknowledging the topic's importance while deferring a deeper discussion is excellent for several reasons:

- Honesty and transparency: it demonstrates respect for students by acknowledging the topic's significance and your commitment to addressing it thoughtfully.
- Time for reflection: it allows you to thoroughly research the topic, ensuring you present accurate and balanced information.
- Student engagement: it encourages students to become active learners by researching the topic independently and forming their own initial perspectives.
- Meaningful discussion: by allowing time for research and reflection, you can facilitate a more in-depth and meaningful discussion when you revisit the topic.

This can be done at the beginning of a lesson or the start of the week, so that it does not feel like it is lingering without it being addressed. In fact, at a conference I led on gendered behaviour policies and toxic masculinity in 2021, one member of the student panel shared that what was most frustrating for them was when teachers did not address 'the elephant in the room', or events and topics that students wanted to talk about. The student commented they were not looking for answers, just for some recognition of the topic.

Equally, it is most important that as a teacher, you address it when it feels most comfortable – and safe – for you, too. You could schedule a specific lesson for the discussion. This could be a dedicated 'current events' lesson or integrated into a relevant unit (e.g. media literacy, social studies). If that's not possible, consider assigning students to research the topic from different sources (news articles, reputable websites, academic journals) and to formulate their own initial thoughts and questions. Follow up with a structured discussion where students share their findings, perspectives and questions. Encourage respectful dialogue and critical thinking.

Although the rise of AI and social media can feel overwhelming and uncertain, what we *can* do in the classroom is help students (and parents) to navigate what they see, and questions they may have, through meaningful and trusting conversations in safe spaces – a meaningful way to override the algorithms.

Making space for social mistakes

A group of Year 13 young men told me that as much as PSHE lessons try to teach them about masculinity, stereotypes and 'good behaviour', the lessons are often outdated, lack clarity and leave little room for failure. One student commented, 'We're allowed to fail academically, but we're not allowed to fail socially.' This makes sense if we think back to young people generally spending more time online than in conversation with one another, in 'real-life' social settings. Online platforms can offer a degree of anonymity, allowing teens to experiment with social interactions and express themselves more freely without the fear of immediate judgment or social repercussions. You don't like a photo, or maybe your reel had little to no engagement? Delete it. Most online interactions allow for more control over the pace and nature of the interaction. Teens can carefully craft their messages and edit media before sending, offering a level of control not always possible in face-to-face situations.

On the other hand, unlike face-to-face interactions, online content, especially images and videos, can be easily shared and potentially go viral, making it difficult to control the spread of social mistakes. Online platforms can be breeding grounds for cyberbullying and online harassment, where social mistakes can be amplified and weaponised against individuals. While online platforms may offer a degree of anonymity, it's important to remember that online actions can have real-world consequences.

Social media and content creation can curate such perfection through aesthetically pleasing posts, which impacts young people, who think they have to be perfect without any room for making mistakes, learning or even asking questions. This can be particularly true of diversity and inclusion, when people are learning about anti-racism, LGBTQ+ communities, religion, and more. Social media then can create spaces where students can learn about the latter and more, without feeling the pressure of asking questions or 'feeling silly' if they don't know something.

The rise of figures like Andrew Tate and others highlights the challenges teachers face in addressing problematic views, such as toxic masculinity. One student shared that they were discouraged from discussing these issues with friends and peers, fearing accusations of 'mansplaining'.[34] This experience underscores the importance of creating safe spaces for open and honest dialogue within the school environment. While inviting external speakers may not always be feasible due to time and resource constraints, schools can still address these issues effectively. Opportunities for critical discussion can be integrated into tutor time, PSHE lessons, debate clubs, and even within relevant subject areas.

More than anything, in the same way that social media has perfectly curated a great deal of aesthetically pleasing context, schools need to curate intentional safe spaces that help provide some balance and room for conversation so that young people have a place to navigate the online world they are consuming. This way, we can ensure they find a true sense of belonging among trusting people who are not necessarily behind a screen.

Why teens remain optimistic about the online world

Remember the Pew survey from the start of this chapter? Given everything we've just covered, why did so many teens still say that the online world was a positive place?

Students can benefit from opportunities for self-expression, mental health support and even strengthened relationships through the use of social media and online platforms.

For teenagers from minoritised backgrounds, the online world can offer unique benefits that may not be as readily available offline. If a student feels marginalised

[34]When a man explains something to someone (typically a woman) in a condescending or patronising matter, often about a subject in which the recipient is equally or more knowledgeable.

and disconnected in a classroom (particularly students with marginalised identities), they are likely to turn to social media and a place where they can find a great deal of connection – even if it is not positive.

Online spaces can provide a sense of community and belonging for teens who may feel isolated or marginalised in their offline lives due to factors like race, ethnicity, sexual orientation or gender identity. They can connect with peers who share similar experiences, find support groups, and access information and resources relevant to their identities. For teens living in rural areas or in communities with limited diversity, online platforms can connect them with peers from diverse backgrounds, expanding their social circles and providing access to different perspectives.

Connecting with others who share similar experiences can boost self-esteem and confidence. Teens can find validation and support within online communities, fostering a sense of belonging and acceptance. For example, a young woman of colour may find inspiration and confidence by connecting with other young women creators and activists online who are challenging racial stereotypes and advocating for social justice. Inspired by youth activists like Greta Thunberg, a new wave of young people are passionately advocating for change across the globe. While the potential for misuse is often highlighted, social media can be a powerful tool for positive change. Young activists are demonstrating this every day by effectively utilising these platforms to raise awareness, mobilise support, and drive meaningful action on a wide range of social and environmental issues.

As well as affirming community, online platforms can connect teens with people from different cultures and backgrounds, providing opportunities to learn about different perspectives, experiences, and ways of life.

Can social media belong in the classroom?

Social media most definitely creates a barrier to psychologically safe classrooms, however, it also reinforces the importance and necessity for psychologically safe classrooms in schools today. Young people may spend a great deal of time 'belonging' online, however, they also spend the dominant part of their days and formative years in the classroom. As teachers, we can confront the issues that arise from social media, through discussion and psychologically safe classrooms where students feel empowered to talk, challenge, question and, most importantly, listen to one another to create a culture of belonging across their school.

Figures like Andrew Tate attract young men by offering what appears to be unconditional acceptance – a space where they don't have to be perfect or measure up to certain standards. But this 'acceptance' often comes with a catch: it validates harmful attitudes while making healthier, more challenging paths to self-growth seem less appealing.

Equally, our students are not *just* on social media: for young people, their teachers, parents and carers, defining time 'online' can be a number of things. It may be gaming, tutoring, doing homework or messaging friends and family. Recognising this broader definition of 'online' is crucial for understanding how technology shapes our students' lives. Importantly, this diverse online landscape also presents incredible opportunities for learning, creativity and social connection. By fostering a positive and supportive digital environment, we can empower our students to thrive in the increasingly interconnected world.

13 Reverse Mentoring and Peer Mentoring

Imagine turning the traditional teacher–student relationship on its head for a moment. That's what reverse mentoring is all about – creating structured opportunities for students to share their insights and experiences with us as teachers. While it might feel uncomfortable at first (after all, we're used to being the experts), the benefits can be transformative. What might this look like in practice?

'Miss, can I explain something?' says Zainab, a Year 11 student who wears a hijab. 'When you taught that poem about identity last week, some of us really wanted to share our experiences, but it felt too personal in front of the whole class.' This kind of feedback is gold. It helps us to understand the invisible barriers some students face and to adapt our teaching accordingly. Maybe next time, we can offer written reflection options alongside class discussion, or create smaller discussion groups where students feel safer sharing. This is reverse mentoring in action.

Traditionally, reverse mentoring refers to early-career professionals mentoring their senior colleagues. The common goal is to promote the professional development of people across different generations and help them to learn from each other, particularly in areas where younger generations may have more expertise. In the 1990s, Jack Welch, CEO of General Electric, used reverse mentoring for junior employees to mentor senior employees about using the internet. The process is now often used to amplify underrepresented voices with senior colleagues, who are in positions of influence and can make the changes needed to create a more equitable workforce.

Why do schools need reverse mentoring?

When I first read about it, I thought that schools do this all the time: through student council, student leadership positions and just by feedback and discussion in the classroom; it's nothing new. However, a more critical lens made me realise that, while schools engage in feedback from students, *who* is it that usually occupies student council and student leadership roles? It's not often underrepresented and minoritised students. Student council and head student roles often go to students who are comfortable with public speaking and usually have the expected grasp of school work and extracurricular activities. These roles are frequently filled by students who do not need intervention or additional support at school. Student elections and recruitment to these roles may be tinged with bias, too: they may rely on a class vote or consideration of 'performance' at school. That's not to say these students are undeserving: they confidently support student voice and amplify many issues that affect the student body. However, their lived experiences may differ significantly from the unheard and minoritised voices at your school. Just as a teacher may struggle to understand a minoritised student's lived experiences or feelings, fellow students might, too.

While schools are an environment where we are constantly talking to students and teachers and getting feedback through the very act of teaching, student councils, form representatives and just plain old conversation, reverse mentoring is a long-term, sustainable relationship between a senior or middle leader and a student, which flips the roles of student and teacher.

When examining any gaps in your 'belonging blueprint' and also thinking about the deeper issues you are trying to address and the students you want to speak to, reverse mentoring can help you to reach these students and, most importantly, it can help these students to reach you. If students feel seen and heard and that their thoughts and suggestions are being put into action, it has a positive impact on their engagement, attendance, sense of belonging, wellbeing and academic success. Reverse mentoring helps to cultivate a school's culture of belonging and diversity of thought.

Implementing reverse mentoring in the classroom

To implement reverse mentoring in your classroom:

1. Choose a year group class you would like to learn from (in an ideal world, this might be every class, but this is a marathon, not a sprint!).
2. Think about the area of classroom practice and the classroom environment in which you would like mentoring. It could be anything from questions you have about the student experience, curriculum, behaviours in the classroom or displays!
3. Think about the voices you don't always hear from. The students you don't really know. Minoritised students. This isn't necessarily your introverted students, but rather the students that you feel you don't understand on a community/lived experience level, for example.
4. Outline clearly the purpose of reverse mentoring. Be transparent and tell the student body what reverse mentoring is designed to do:

'I would like to be reverse mentored by my students! You will be my mentor and I will be your mentee. There are a few areas of my classroom practice that I want your advice on. Reverse mentoring aims to amplify the voices of students I don't often hear from and

student experiences I don't know much about. I want to improve and strengthen all my students' experiences so that every student I teach feels seen and heard and has a fair experience in the classroom. For this project, I'm particularly interested in being mentored by a student who is xxx. Please come and have a chat with me to find out more!'

Speaking to parents about reverse mentoring

You can share the opportunity with parents – be honest and transparent. While you may get whataboutisms and some parents wondering why their children are not a priority group for this project, I find the following explanations can help:

'Reverse mentoring is an intervention strategy. Intervention is a strategy implemented by schools to reduce inequalities in educational outcomes. We will focus on working with X students, while also providing additional tailored opportunities for other students during their time at school.

At our school, we want to ensure all students have an equal opportunity to succeed. We've noticed that some students from [...] may face additional challenges in reaching their full academic potential. We also recognise that for the past 3–5 years, our student leadership teams have not been representative of our diverse student population. We want to hear from underrepresented students so that we can work towards the success of every student.

I'm sure you can appreciate we have the very best interests of all students in mind. Understandably, every student has different needs and experiences at school. As teachers, we want to understand the experiences of all of our students fully and to empower their voices. This is a great opportunity for students to lead the way in improving diverse student experiences.'

Reverse mentoring is a great way to meet the ongoing demands of leadership and workplace development, allowing students to gain professional experience, build their confidence, and work collaboratively with their teachers on finding solutions and addressing areas of development within education. They can add it to their CV, social media platforms, and more.

Implementing reverse mentoring across the school

While student councils serve an important purpose, reverse mentoring offers something different – a chance for deep, one-to-one dialogue that can transform both individual experiences and wider school culture. I've seen this work particularly well when we take time to prepare both teachers and students for their roles.

Before launching into reverse mentoring, we need to lay some groundwork. Think of it like building a bridge – both sides need solid foundations. For students who'll be taking on the mentor role, this means developing specific skills and understanding clear boundaries.

First, let's talk about mentoring skills. Remember, we're not asking students to become mini-teachers or counsellors. Instead, we're helping them understand how to share their experiences constructively. This might mean practising how to give feedback respectfully or learning to focus on specific situations rather than general complaints. Equally important is the contract – not a formal legal document, but a clear agreement about how the mentoring relationship will work. In my experience, this works best when both mentor and mentee contribute to setting the boundaries.

Questions to explore together might include:

- 'How often should we meet?'
- *'What topics are within bounds for our discussions?'*
- *'How will we handle disagreements?'*
- *'What does success look like for both of us?'*

This preparation might seem like extra work, but it's an investment that pays off in more meaningful conversations and actionable insights. It also models the kind of professional relationship-building that students will encounter in their future careers.

Let's clarify what student-to-teacher mentoring truly means. When students mentor their teachers, they're creating valuable opportunities to collaborate and share their lived experiences in a safe space. This not only helps to build a sense of belonging for themselves but also for students like them. Through this process, teachers can learn and implement changes – some might be small adjustments to classroom practice, while others could lead to bigger institutional shifts.

However, it's important to be clear about what this mentoring relationship *isn't*. While students might raise concerns, this isn't meant to be a complaints forum. Nor is it a way to get extra academic support from teachers. And while the experience might indeed look good on a UCAS application or CV, this shouldn't be the primary motivation for getting involved. The focus should remain on creating meaningful dialogue that benefits the whole school community. That may sound cynical – perhaps it is. However, it is important to be as transparent as you can about the boundaries you need for reverse mentoring to be successful.

Reverse mentoring is a sensitive relationship that needs to be managed and navigated with care. You may choose to invest in formal reverse mentoring training, or work with a practitioner, school, or teachers and students who have prior experience in reverse mentoring. I piloted a reverse mentoring programme at Buckinghamshire New University and have also learned from the excellent work that Dr Jenni Jones is leading on at the University of Wolverhampton for a postgraduate reverse mentoring scheme. The Reverse Mentoring Practice is a great place to start and Patrice Gordon's book, *Reverse Mentoring*, can also be applied to the classroom.

Here are a few strategies for teachers who wish to initiate reverse mentoring within their own classrooms or departments:

- **Start small and build:** begin with a small pilot programme involving a few mentor–mentee pairs.
- **Focus on building relationships:** prioritise building strong relationships between mentors and mentees.
- **Regularly evaluate and adjust:** evaluate the programme's effectiveness with colleagues, students and school governors and adjust as necessary. You will need to schedule regular reflective feedback sessions, perhaps one a term, to do this.
- **Share successes and challenges:** share your experiences and learning with other teachers to encourage their participation and support.

In any case, it is important to understand that reverse mentoring cannot work in isolation. This is a common criticism of such initiatives. To be successful, it must be integrated into the school culture, which should value diversity of thought, encourage feedback, support open conversations, promote collaboration, and foster co-creation.

I have spoken about reverse mentoring to different teachers and headteachers, and while it 'sounds great' (which it is), it is essential to take others along the journey with you. Building a culture of belonging in your classroom can be possible as an individual teacher, but it is much easier, more sustainable and healthier if reverse mentoring is at the centre of your school values and ethos.

TIP

Discuss the potential benefits of reverse mentoring with colleagues during staff meetings, coffee breaks or informal gatherings. Share the programme with your headteacher or deputy headteacher and seek their support and guidance. Establish a dedicated forum or online platform for mentors and mentees to share their experiences, ask questions and exchange ideas. Schedule regular check-ins with participating staff members to monitor progress, address any challenges and celebrate successes.

Whole-school buy-in will also reassure marginalised communities (of staff and students) that interventions like this are not tokenistic or superficial. Instead, there is a genuine desire to understand and listen to hidden voices, take action, and make the necessary changes needed to create a culture of belonging and inclusion.

Alumni mentoring

Alumni embody the achievements of their university and signify what students can accomplish and become as a result of their university experience. Students are also a representation of their school, and they keep the reputation and values of the school alive throughout their adulthood and working life. Many schools do this already, but if your school doesn't, here are some ways to maintain positive relationships with your school alumni to support a values-led, psychologically safe school:

- Promote mentoring schemes with alumni and ensure they represent your student body. Could pairings or groupings be arranged to share similar lived experiences or backgrounds?
- Invite student alumni back to speak to students in assemblies, and informally in a classroom setting, at lunchtime, or on a Zoom call. Make the environment comfortable and appropriate for different groups of students.
- Be transparent with alumni and let them know which groups of students you are trying to engage and support. Is it SEND students? Pakistani or Bangladeshi boys? Black, African or Caribbean students? Students who would be the first in the family to attend university? This clarity will likely make the relationships more purposeful and beneficial for the mentee.

Buddying

A while ago I asked a group of male students, 'How do we overcome toxic masculinity?'. Their suggestions were very practical and in some ways, simple: 'Put us in front of them.'

Without wanting to offend me, a few male students said it helps if students can speak to people they identify with and relate to. No offence taken! In a secondary school setting, reach out to your Sixth Form male students to lead and support small group conversations with younger students. Introduce a buddy system, so that younger students have a buddy in the older year groups they are able talk to. Maybe once a fortnight, they could arrange to meet a student one to one during form time, in the library or school canteen.

The latter examples have been implemented at a few schools I have worked at, and I am sure are common practice in many schools. It is important to maintain and sustain these relationships over a period of time; as opposed to students just having a buddy for one term, why not trial it for a year? After all, we often teach the same class all year round and we know how much time it takes to build trust – why would it be any different for a buddy?

These conversations and buddy structures can be built around psychological safety and trust. It is essential to empower students to take the lead in these spaces. While we may not fully agree with their approaches, they can still be effective if they are based on a sensible rationale that aligns with your school values and fosters a culture of belonging.

CASE STUDY

Leading small group discussions

It has been over a year since Andrew Tate highlighted the discussions surrounding masculinity, particularly in schools, as well as the concept of 'toxic masculinity'.

Interventions like this led to the school creating a whole-school, student-led charter to address external influences on the school environment proactively. The charter was led by Dan Colquhoun and was developed by students and staff working together to identify behaviours, attitudes and values all students should model to create a positive and safe environment. The charter was shared with parents, carers and the school community via the school's main communication channels and it is displayed around the school. Time was also dedicated to supporting staff to implement the charter during CPD sessions and INSET days.

Peer mentoring

I consulted with former headteacher and education consultant Frances Akinde about how to foster a culture of inclusion and belonging for SEND and neurodivergent students in our classrooms.

'How can teachers educate students without lived experiences or awareness of SEND to be allies and respect one another?'

'It's crucial to educate all students about neurodiversity and SEND to foster a culture of respect and understanding. Peer mentorship programmes can encourage "neurotypical" students to support their neurodiverse classmates. Open discussions about diversity and inclusion can also help address any stigmas head on. It's about creating a community where everyone feels valued and understood.'

'Do you have examples of situations in schools that nurtured safety and belonging for students, or addressed uncomfortable situations for SEND students? How did you overcome these uncomfortable situations?'

'Take, for example, schools that have set up their own Autism Resource Bases/provisions. They provide students with autism the support they need while allowing them to participate in mainstream classes, striking a balance between specialised support and inclusion. Another great initiative is the "neuro-ambassadors" programme, where neurodiverse students are trained to educate their peers about neurodiversity. This not only empowers the neurodiverse students but also fosters a more inclusive school culture.'

As Frances notes, peer mentoring, when implemented thoughtfully, creates powerful networks of support within our schools. Students develop leadership skills and empathy while mentors gain fresh perspectives on their teaching practice. These relationships help to build the inclusive, understanding environment that allows all students to thrive.

Yet for these mentoring programmes to truly succeed, they need to be part of a broader commitment to student advocacy across the whole school. In the next chapter, we'll explore how teachers can take the insights gained from peer mentoring and use them to champion student needs at an institutional level.

14 Advocating for Students in a Whole-School Context

During Ramadan, a group of Sixth Form students approached me, and the school's DEI lead, with concerns about prayer and reflection spaces. I reminded students of the dedicated prayer space in the school. While students made use of the space, they found that the space filled up quickly and it was inconvenient due to its distance from the Sixth Form hub, often leading to delays and missed lessons. The limited capacity of the prayer room, and the frequent congestion of school toilets during break and lunchtimes, created additional challenges for students fulfilling their religious obligations.

Students had provided me with constructive knowledge: information that has a tangible and often nuanced impact on their experiences, something only they experience. I *listened* to the students and realised that while the school had created a space for worship, there were practical obstacles (barriers) at play: they were trying to attend extracurricular sessions while aiming to fulfil their prayer obligations too.

I asked students, 'What would be helpful in these situations?' They proposed utilising vacant classrooms closer to the Sixth Form area for prayer when needed and suggested using the reception toilets, which were generally less crowded, for ablutions.

I presented these options to senior leadership and found several suitable classrooms. This information was shared with teachers, addressing concerns about health and safety and establishing clear guidelines for their use. All questions were collaboratively addressed, with staff on regular duty in those areas asked to check on the classrooms. These classrooms were designated as quiet spaces for students to use as needed, not exclusively for prayer. This approach aligned with the school's inclusive values and was communicated to the entire school community to ensure awareness and respect for these designated spaces. Overall, the small intervention and adjustment was a compassionate and constructive response to student needs, having a great impact on Muslim student belonging at school.

What ifs and whataboutisms

Naturally, some colleagues raised concerns. 'What if students misuse these spaces?' 'What if too many students congregate in these areas?' 'What if this sets a precedent for other student groups to request dedicated spaces?'

All of these concerns are valid and there is no denying that all of this may happen! However, it's important to remember the specific request: Sixth Form students sought access to nearby classrooms for brief prayer periods (5–10 minutes) and the use of reception toilets for ablutions during Ramadan. This request reflects a genuine need to balance academic and religious obligations. By addressing this specific need, the school demonstrated a commitment to student wellbeing and inclusivity.

In this situation, it is clear that student voice has been considered and an agreeable option for the school and the students has been reached. A communication plan, linked to the school's values, has been shared with all students and teachers, explaining a clear rationale for the adjustments. Equally, boundaries and expectations, based on trust and compassion, have been shared too.

There are other situations such as drama rehearsals, lunchtime clubs, wet play or revision classes, where similar 'whataboutisms' about classrooms may creep in. We must ask ourselves: Are our reservations about these specific requests proportionate to our responses to other requests for classroom space? Do we apply the same level of scrutiny to all requests, regardless of the group making the request?

For instance, a teacher might say:

- *'A revision class will always be supervised because teachers are around and there are more students there.'*
- *'Wet play is for all students.'*
- *'Students have always needed classrooms for rehearsals and their projects; that is very different.'*

It is important to understand the underlying reasons for whataboutisms. Whataboutisms often attempt to deflect attention from the issue at hand by introducing irrelevant comparisons or raising counterarguments that may or may not be valid. By understanding the underlying motivations, we can more effectively address the concerns raised.

1 **Use the school's values to support your argument** If your school claims to be a supportive and inclusive school for all students, resisting measures like prayer spaces, LGBTQ+ spaces and the use of pronouns directly contradicts these values.
2 **Focus on the positive outcomes** It can help to explain exactly how the space or school rule will be implemented and who it will have a *positive* impact on – not a negative. Often, resistance to change focuses on potential negative consequences. Instead of getting caught up in debating the validity of those concerns, let's focus on the positive outcomes. Let's show how these changes can actually benefit everyone. In this example, we can explain how providing prayer spaces can:

- make students feel more comfortable and supported
- show that we value and respect the diverse needs of our students
- create a more inclusive and welcoming school environment for all.

3 **Remain compassionate and empathetic** Don't fall into the trap of responding to the whataboutery. Instead, focus on *why* adapting the policy, rule or practice will benefit the students and staff in question. When you fall into the trap of thinking more about the whataboutery than the problem at hand, the other person has won.

4 **Be curious** Often, whataboutisms arise from a predisposition to say 'no'. Instead of immediately dismissing concerns, let's approach them with curiosity. Instead of seeing them as obstacles, let's view them as opportunities for discussion and exploration. We can ask ourselves: *'Could we approach this issue differently?' 'What if we experimented with a new approach?' 'What have other schools done successfully in similar situations?'* All of these questions can be posed curiously, creating room for a conversation, healthy debate and disagreement. This approach is far more likely to lead to positive outcomes than simply dismissing concerns or getting drawn into unproductive arguments.

Advocacy in simple conversations

Picture the scene:

Teacher 1: *[interrupting a meeting]*	*Hi, sorry, just wondering if you have a minute for a quick question?*
Teacher 2:	*Sure, come on in. What's up?*
Teacher 1:	*OK, great! Just wondering – a few Sixth Form students have come to see me about prayer spaces during Ramadan and…*
Teacher 2: *[interrupting]*	*…ah yes, we've got the space at the top of the next block for them.*
Teacher 1:	*Yes, they know about that, but they're finding it a bit inconvenient. The prayer room is quite far from the Sixth Form block, and it takes them a while to get there, especially when they have to rush back for lunchtime club activities.*
Teacher 2:	*Really? It's not that far – everyone else manages to use it and we've not had any complaints.*
Teacher 1:	*It might be OK for students closer to the prayer room, but for the Sixth Formers, it's a bit of a trek. They were*

wondering if we could find some alternative spaces closer to their area.

Teacher 2: *[exasperated]* *Right OK, so what do they want?*

Teacher 1: *They'd really like some prayer spaces near their Sixth Form area, which I think is a great idea and means they can still get to their lunchtime clubs on time.*

Teacher 2: *But what about the other students? Shouldn't all students have access to classrooms during breaks and lunch?*

Teacher 1: *Well, these wouldn't be general study spaces. These would be designated spaces for prayer periods during Ramadan. And there are plenty of other areas in the school for students to hang out.*

Teacher 2: *I don't know. What about monitoring them while they're in there? We don't have capacity for that.*

Teacher 1: *I understand. We could maybe designate a couple of classrooms near the Sixth Form for short prayer periods during Ramadan, and have lunchtime supervisors keep an eye on them. It wouldn't be for the whole break; just for short periods. Or we could explore some other options, like staggering breaktimes for different year groups or finding alternative spaces within the Sixth Form block itself?*

Teacher 2: *OK, I'll need to think about it. I don't want this to cause any disruptions or extra work.*

Teacher 1: *Not at all; if anything, it will build the students' sense of connection and positivity with the school, which is a good thing. I don't think we can see some student requests as disruption and others as not. They've also asked to use the visitor toilets…*

Teacher 2: *No, I don't know about that. The visitor toilets are for visitors, and we need to keep them available.*

Teacher 1: *Yes, but the main school toilets get quite crowded, especially during break and lunch. The visitor toilets might offer a bit more privacy and convenience, especially if someone needs to take off their hijab.*

Teacher 2: *I'll have to think about it. I'll speak to [Head of Year/ Senior Leadership] and see what they think.*

Teacher 1: *Thanks, I appreciate you taking the time to talk about this.*

This exchange is a great example of advocacy in action. Even though Teacher 1 didn't have all the answers and wasn't necessarily in a position to make changes, they didn't simply dismiss the students' concerns. Instead, they listened carefully to their suggestions and shared their thoughts with a colleague.

By creating space for open discussion and exploring potential solutions, Teacher 1 was actively contributing to a culture of belonging and inclusion within the school.

In this scenario, classroom spaces were agreed and so was use of the visitors' toilets during Ramadan. To some this may seem like a brilliant step; to others it may not go far enough (why *just* during Ramadan?), but every small step forward matters. It shows students that their voices are heard and valued. A step in a direction that advocates 'micro' changes can have a 'macro' impact on students, their sense of belonging and connection. Equally, as staff begin to see the positive outcomes of these inclusive practices, they're more likely to embrace similar initiatives in the future.

15 Conducting a Belonging and Behaviour Audit

Let's talk honestly about behaviour policies. Yes, they exist to keep everyone safe and create an orderly learning environment. But as any teacher knows, applying these policies while honouring student identity and maintaining belonging isn't always straightforward. When a student's cultural expression seems to conflict with uniform rules, or when traditional consequences might affect different students differently, we face real dilemmas.

I am very aware that behaviour policies, uniform policies, and policies and processes that impact student identity and actions can be contentious. They often lead to very emotive responses, which is understandable as we all have different approaches, views, beliefs, and so on, to behaving and being!

You can't please everyone and no matter how much voice a teacher, leader or governing body collects, there will always be objections, disagreements and non-compliance. And let's face it, we've all been there – quietly disagreeing with a rule while still having to enforce it.

Consider this example: a student repeatedly arrives late because they're helping younger siblings get ready for school. The standard policy might call for detention, but is that the most effective response? This is where belonging-informed practice comes in.

It is important to reflect and consider whether the behaviour policy and strategy takes an inclusive, fair, safe and equitable approach. Just because a policy exists, doesn't mean it's truly working for everyone. As teachers in the classroom, walking the corridors, you are (usually) the ones who see the policy 'in action' more than the people who write them. Audits are usually carried out by governance and leadership, but they should be carried out by those impacted by the policies most: you and your students.

Grab a cup of tea and pull out a copy of your school and/or departmental behaviour policy. We're going to do a little audit – not to find fault, but to make sure it's truly reflecting the values of our school and supporting all our students. All schools operate differently and may take different approaches to what a behaviour policy looks like and how you, as a teacher, are expected to use it, hence I have not included an example here. As you read through your behaviour policy, conduct a belonging audit, using the table below:

QUESTION	EVIDENCE	WHAT IS THE IMPACT (POSITIVE AND NEGATIVE)?
Has the policy been adapted to include approaches to suit the needs of SEND and neurodivergent students?		
Does the behaviour policy include approaches for students in care, in temporary housing or experiencing homelessness, or for refugee students and vulnerable students?		
Does the behaviour policy take a trauma-informed response*?		
Does the behaviour policy include clear and transparent information about consequences and sanctions?		
Is the behaviour policy linked to the school's anti-racism, gender-equity and anti-bullying policies?		
Have student voices been included in policy development?		
Have parent and carer voices been included in policy development?		
Have support staff voices (lunchtime controllers, reception staff, canteen staff, site staff) been consulted?		
Is the rationale for the policy clearly explained?		
Is the policy shared with all parents in a variety of formats?		

QUESTION	EVIDENCE	WHAT IS THE IMPACT (POSITIVE AND NEGATIVE)?
BEHAVIOUR TRENDS		
If your school rewards positive behaviour, which students are consistently and regularly achieving these rewards in your classroom? What's their story?		
Which students are consistently or regularly not meeting the behaviour policy criteria in your classroom? What's their story?		
What trends and patterns do you notice about behaviour in your classroom?		

* See Chapter 11 and the Glossary on pages 171–74.

This isn't about nit-picking or complaining. It's about taking a closer look at how our policies are actually working in practice and making sure they're truly supporting the success and wellbeing of every single student.

How to approach the belonging and behaviour audit

You may need two or three beverages as you may want to complete the audit in more than one sitting. You may also want to do this with a few colleagues: in fact, I'd recommend it. Choose colleagues from various departments and include support staff, too, so that you can discuss behaviour and your students from different perspectives. If the opportunity arises, you could speak to your senior leaders about a whole-school project and auditing the policy with students.

The audit may feel overwhelming, particularly if you don't find the evidence you are looking for. There may be some questions for which you have no evidence or answers because it might be that your school doesn't teach those students at present and has limited history with that student context. That's OK. An audit allows schools and teachers to reflect and revise policies. The audit is not a test; it is a reflection tool. If there are gaps and further questions arise, that's brilliant! Those questions and gaps offer opportunities for discussion and the implementation of change.

The last column asks you to reflect on the impact of equality and belonging for every student. There might be evidence for every question. That column then encourages you to think about the potential positive and negative consequences and implications for different students. For example:

- If adaptations have been made for SEND and neurodivergent students, this should positively impact their feelings of safety and belonging. However, have teachers been given the appropriate training and development to adapt the policy and processes? Have these adaptations been communicated with all parents and students to establish a culture of belonging and inclusion and to avoid any misunderstandings and 'whataboutery'?
- You may have no refugee students in your school or perhaps only one or two students in care. However, every student matters and if their voices and needs are absent in the behaviour policy, this can significantly impact awarding, attendance, progress and wellbeing. It is important to proactively address behaviour to support every student.
- Support staff may not have been consulted about the policy. However, if support staff are 'on duty' at break and lunchtimes, they will definitely have to manage and navigate both positive and problematic situations. They will have different relationships with students too. Their input and behaviour management can not only positively affect student wellbeing and inclusion, but it can also support teachers in the classroom too. If a behaviour incident, for example, racial slurs, is heard at lunchtime and not appropriately managed, this will undoubtedly enter the classroom in the latter half of the day. Addressing these risks, and putting inclusive training and development in place for support staff, empowers support staff and nurtures a culture of safety and understanding for all students too.

The final three questions require a great deal of reflection, which may feel uncomfortable. This is because we have gone from auditing the behaviour policy to reflecting on our own actions and implementation of the behaviour policy in our classrooms. When I was teaching, this was one of my favourite things to do. It really made me think about my relationships with my students and what I knew about them. It made me reflect on how my teaching practices might be impacting students with different personalities, learning styles and backgrounds. For example, I considered how my teaching style might affect introverted and extroverted students, students from different cultural backgrounds, and even how my own mood or energy levels might influence my interactions with students on different days of the week. It's not an easy process and one you can approach in stages. You may not be empowered to make major changes to the whole-school behaviour policy, but you *can* make small changes to your own classroom practice and inclusive behaviour choices.

The belonging and behaviour audit (BAB for short) is a big one, however, it is one you can break down and present to various staff members to complete in a collegiate and collaborative manner. You may focus on a few questions for your classroom, and make pragmatic decisions and changes that enhance a culture of belonging that is *within your control.* If there is anything else that you notice and highlight, *pass it on.* That isn't to pass on 'the problem(!)' but to acknowledge that nurturing a culture of belonging in behaviour management also requires a whole-school approach and cannot be the sole responsibility of one individual.

There is often a social media storm around behaviour policies and rules. It usually leads to binary viewpoints, that don't consider individual school circumstances or create room for nuanced discussions. Social media can be a great space to learn for teachers, but it can also create quite the ride. Accounting for belonging, compassion and empathy in behaviour policy does not *exclude* or mitigate accountability for unsafe and unacceptable behaviour. Instead, the BAB audit and proactive thinking about belonging and inclusion in your behaviour policies ensure that all students and staff with diverse lived experiences are safe. It ensures we take a proactive and positive approach to behaviour, rather than a deficit approach.

Detentions, toilet rules and mobile phone policies may work in your school, and they may be working well. The BAB audit encourages you to question whether these rules and guidelines are enabling learning, achievement and wellbeing for every student, or whether you begin to notice a trend about the students who repeatedly break the rules? Do you notice a trend in students consistently achieving 'good behaviour' points, great progress and success? While the audit doesn't provide answers, it creates space for you as teachers and as a school to find answers and approaches that work for you and your context.

Policies and practices of allyship

We look at behaviour policies on page 157, which will also take the LGBTQ+ community, along with other minoritised communities, into account when conducting your BAB audit. It is extremely important to be consistent with this. Students are most likely to experience anti-LGBTQ+ behaviour in the form of microaggressions, bullying and teasing. These experiences can lead to students turning inward and feeling isolated. David quite rightly says, 'Being LGBTQ+ is not a safeguarding risk; homophobia is.' This powerful statement applies to gender inequity, antisemitism, Islamophobia, race inequalities, religious inequalities, socioeconomic disadvantages and more. Policies and practices that place inclusion and belonging at the heart comply with our responsibility to safeguard students, too.

Allyship ensures that every student feels safe in the classroom. Every teacher does this almost instinctively as part of everyday classroom practice. While classroom safety is often written into school values, rules and behaviour practices, we may need to adapt the latter to ally with the students we teach. Several situations can arise that might challenge a teacher's allyship. For example:

- You might need to adapt your seating plan to accommodate neurodivergent students or students with hidden disabilities who occasionally need to leave the classroom. How do I explain this to a classroom where most students do *not* need to leave?
- Uniform rules, which often include rules and expectations about physical appearance, may disadvantage students with Afro-Caribbean hairstyles or who wear the hijab, the kippah or the kara. How do I know what these are, to adapt to classroom expectations?
- A register does not often contain information about pronouns. How can I ensure we are addressing students (and that they are addressing each other) accurately without causing offence or drawing unwanted attention?
- Slavery is the topic of study and certain students are aiming what they regard as 'banter' towards Black and Asian students. How do I manage this appropriately, particularly when the students targeted tell me 'not to worry about it'?
- It is Ramadan, and Muslim students are asking if they can complete a piece of homework or a test on a different day. How can I enable this without it being unfair to other students?
- A student has asked not to sit near any boys in class as it goes against their religious beliefs. How can I enable this in a secular school and classroom setting?
- A student has said they have had their nose pierced for religious reasons, but this goes against our school policy. How can I allow this in school?
- A student has asked not to participate in music lessons because it goes against their religion and they have said it is not a mandatory part of the school curriculum either. As their music teacher, what do I do?

In each of these situations, teachers can demonstrate allyship by actively listening to the student's needs, exploring potential solutions together, and advocating for their wellbeing. A helpful reflection model for teachers could involve these steps:

- Instead of rushing to respond, take a moment to process the situation. Give yourself time to reflect on the student's needs and consider the best course of action. It doesn't have to be immediate.

- Review the school's behaviour policy and expectations – remind yourself that all students have the right to feel safe and that bullying or belittling behaviour will not be tolerated.
- Talk to the student directly – discuss their concerns with them openly and honestly. Reiterate the school's expectations for behaviour while also exploring flexible solutions that meet their individual needs.
- Collaborate with parents, carers and other teachers too – come up with a collaborative arrangement that ensures everyone is seen and heard. By working together, we can find solutions that benefit all stakeholders – the student, the teacher, and the school as a whole.

CASE STUDY

Adapting my behaviour approach

Several years ago, I was teaching a GCSE class with a high proportion of male students, many of whom were of South Asian heritage. These students were often seen as 'high flyers' in the school. I generally had positive relationships with them, but one student consistently struggled with homework.

Despite my efforts to enforce the school's behaviour policy – which I believe is generally fair and inclusive – and offer extensions, the situation wasn't improving. This student, despite demonstrating excellent engagement and understanding in class, consistently missed homework deadlines. I realised that simply applying the standard consequences wasn't addressing the root of the problem.

I began to notice a pattern. Students who consistently handed in their homework, achieved high grades and participated actively in extracurricular activities, often came from stable home environments. This particular student, however, was living in temporary accommodation and facing significant challenges at home. While his family provided loving support, their circumstances were undoubtedly impacting his ability to complete homework.

One day, I had a conversation with him about his challenges. Instead of focusing on the missed assignments, I focused on finding a solution that worked for him. We agreed that he would come to my classroom early in the morning, before school started, and I would help him with his work (note: this isn't to suggest teachers need to get to school extra early; we agreed he was able to come into school when I arrived for my working day too). I helped him to create a revision timetable and, for my subject, a 'need to know and learn list'. There was no point chasing the multiple pieces of missed homework. Maybe it was my organisation, but it felt like a mess forcing this student to complete a backlog of work when we'd reached the stage where I needed them to revise and get the exam essay skills right. You may disagree with this when thinking about applying a behaviour policy consistently and 'equally' across all students, however for me, I was adapting my approach to help this student succeed.

It wasn't always easy, and there were days when both of us were tired. I remember the student saying to me, 'I'm only doing this for you, miss!' and thinking he's kind of missing the point! On reflection, it felt that we were working together through 'behavioural' issues that were, in essence, beyond his control and mine. Instead, we did what was in our control to get him through their exams. It felt like we were working together to overcome this obstacle, rather than simply enforcing a rule.

Although we didn't make any changes to the school's overall behaviour policy, this experience taught me the importance of adapting my teaching practices to meet the individual needs of my students. It reinforced the idea that a one-size-fits-all approach to behaviour management rarely works. In this particular case, by providing individualised support and understanding, I was able to help this student to succeed academically, despite the challenges he faced outside of school. He eventually went on to study A Level English Literature, which was a testament to his resilience and a reminder of the importance of adapting our teaching to support the unique needs of each student.

Conclusion: Beginning the Journey

Every time a student takes a risk in your classroom – whether that's answering a difficult question, sharing a personal story, or admitting they don't understand – they're telling us something important about belonging. These moments don't happen by accident. They happen because teachers like you have intentionally created spaces where students feel valued, capable and safe enough to be vulnerable.

Teaching has always been more than just delivering content. At its heart, it's about nurturing young people who feel valued, capable and ready to engage with the world. Creating genuine belonging in our classrooms isn't a destination we arrive at, but rather a continuous journey of learning, adjusting and growing alongside our students. The classroom, then, is not just a physical space, but a culture that we co-create and nurture with our students and fellow colleagues.

Throughout this book, we've explored frameworks and approaches for tackling difficult conversations and creating inclusive spaces. You may have noticed that I haven't always provided rigid scripts or universal solutions – because there aren't any. Every classroom is unique, every student brings their own lived experience, and every conversation about belonging will unfold differently.

What I have aimed to provide is a foundation of understanding and a toolkit for approaching these vital conversations with confidence. From examining our own biases and assumptions, to creating psychologically safe spaces, to implementing practical strategies for curriculum reform and peer support – these are all building blocks that you can adapt to your specific context.

Some days, you'll get it wrong. There will be moments of discomfort, uncertainty and possibly even tension. This is OK and, indeed, necessary. Real growth – both for teachers and students – often happens in these moments of productive discomfort. What matters is our willingness to stay engaged, to listen deeply and to keep learning, with the intention to create a culture of belonging, safety and inclusion.

Remember that you don't need to be perfect to make a difference. Every small step towards creating more inclusive spaces matters. Whether it's learning to pronounce names correctly, using pronouns in email communication with students, making space for diverse perspectives in your curriculum or simply acknowledging when you don't have all the answers – these actions signal to students that they are valued members of your classroom community.

The conversations you begin may ripple out beyond your classroom walls. Students who feel genuinely seen and heard often become advocates for inclusion in other spaces. The belonging you nurture in your classroom can help to shape how your students engage with the wider world.

As you close this book and return to your classroom, I encourage you to start small but think big. Choose one area where you feel ready to make a change. Perhaps it's opening one of the further reading books suggested at the end of this book, auditing your curriculum materials, speaking to a colleague about what you've read and what they do in their classroom, setting up a peer mentoring programme, or simply opening up more spaces for authentic dialogue. Build from there, learning and adapting as you go.

Most importantly, remember that you're not alone in this work. Connect with colleagues, seek support when needed and share your experiences. The journey towards creating truly inclusive classrooms is one we make together, step by step, conversation by conversation.

Your students need you to be brave enough to start these conversations, even if you don't feel fully prepared. They need you to model what it looks like to engage with complexity, to acknowledge mistakes, and to keep growing. By picking up this book, you've already shown that you're ready to take on this challenge.

The future of education lies not just in what we teach, but in how we create spaces, together with our students, where every student can truly belong. Thank you for being part of this vital work. Now, take what resonates from these pages and begin your own journey towards fostering genuine belonging in your classroom.

Suggested Reading List

Books on belonging and education

Ali, H. (2021). *Her Allies: A Practical Toolkit to Help Men Lead Through Advocacy.* Neem Tree Press.

Brown, B. (2021). *Atlas of the Heart: Mapping Meaningful Connection and the Language of Human Experience.* Random House.

Cohen, G. L. (2022). *Belonging: The Science of Creating Connection and Building Trust.* W.W. Norton & Company.

Haidt, J. (2024). *The Anxious Generation: How the Great Rewiring of Childhood Is Causing an Epidemic of Mental Illness.* Penguin Press.

Wilson, H. and Kara, B. (2021). *Diverse Educators: A Manifesto.* John Catt Educational.

Books on race and education

Akala. (2019). *Natives: Race and Class in the Ruins of Empire.* Two Roads.

Asika, U. (2020). *Bringing Up Race: How to Raise a Kind Child in a Prejudiced World.* Yellow Kite.

Asika, U. (2023). *Raising Boys Who Do Better: A Hopeful Guide for a New Generation.* DK.

Banaji, M. R. and Greenwald, A. G. (2013). *Blindspot: Hidden Biases of Good People.* Delacorte Press.

Boakye, J. (2023). *Race Unlisted: A Journey Through Britain's Hidden History.* Dialogue Books.

Coates, T. (2015). *Between the World and Me.* Spiegel & Grau.

Holding, M. (2021). *Why We Kneel, How We Rise.* Simon & Schuster UK.

Kara, B. (2020). *The Diverse Curriculum: A Practical Guide.* John Catt Educational.

Kendi, I. X. (2019). *How to Be an Antiracist.* One World.

Modood, T. (2013). *Multiculturalism: A Civic Idea.* Polity Press.

Oluo, I. (2018). *So You Want to Talk About Race.* Seal Press.

Olusoga, D. (2016). *Black and British: A Forgotten History.* Pan Macmillan.

Shafak, E. (2024). *There Are Rivers in the Sky.* Viking.

Tatum, B. D. (2017). *Why Are All the Black Kids Sitting Together in the Cafeteria? And Other Conversations About Race.* Basic Books.

Thomas, A. (2022). *Representation Matters: How to Create an Inclusive Classroom.* Bloomsbury Education.

Books on psychological safety

Edmondson, A. C. (2012). *Teaming: How Organisations Learn, Innovate, and Compete in the Knowledge Economy*. Jossey-Bass.

Edmondson, A. C. (2018). *The fearless organization: Creating psychological safety in the workplace for learning, innovation, and growth*. John Wiley & Sons.

Books on gender and equality

Bates, L. (2020). *Men Who Hate Women: From Incels to Pickup Artists*. Simon & Schuster.

Bergdorf. M. (2023). *Transitional*. Bloomsbury Tonic.

Boakye, J. and Chetty, D. (2022). *What is Masculinity? Why Does it Matter? And Other Big Questions*. Wayland.

Brassington, J. and Brett, A. (2023). *Pride and Progress: Making Schools LGBTQ+ Inclusive Spaces*. Crown House Publishing.

Harris, S. and Morley, K. (2025). *Tackling Poverty and Disadvantage in Schools*. Bloomsbury Education.

Books on honest conversations

Akinde, F. (2023). *Be an Ally, not a Bystander: Allyship lessons for 7-12-year olds*. Jessica Kingsley Publishers.

Gordon, P. (2020). *Reverse Mentoring: Removing Barriers and Building Belonging in the Workplace*. Human Lens Publishing.

Imani, B. (2021). *Read This to Get Smarter: About Race, Class, Gender, Disability & More*. Ten Speed Press.

Spector, N. (2023). *Say More About That: ...And Other Ways to Speak Up, Push Back, and Advocate for Yourself and Others*. Simon & Schuster.

Syed, M. (2023). *What Do You Think? How to Agree to Disagree and Still Be Friends*. Sourcebooks.

Books about SEND

Allen, G., & Brady, J. (2018). *The Inclusive Classroom: Transformative Strategies for Reaching All Students*. Bloomsbury Publishing.

Ali, A. (2022). *SEND in Schools: A Practical Guide*. Sage Publications.

Resources for teachers

AllSides Media – www.allsides.com
Big Talk cards – https://makebigtalk.app
The Black Curriculum – www.theblackcurriculum.com
Common Sense Media – www.commonsensemedia.org
Cosmos Ltd – www.cosmosltd.uk
Diverse Educators – www.diverseeducators.co.uk
Learning for Justice – www.learningforjustice.org
News Literacy Project – www.newslit.org
The Global Equality Collective – www.gec.education

Reports and research

Dirrane, S. and Dempsey, L. (2023). *The Educational Experiences of the Traveller Community and Impact of Traveller-focused Initiatives: A Qualitative Study*. Educational Research.
Ofcom. (2022). Children and Parents: *Media Use and Attitudes Report 2022*. Ofcom.
Ofcom. (2022). *Children's Media Lives Study*. Ofcom.
Pearson. (2019). *Diversity and Inclusion in Schools Report*. Pearson Education.
Pew Research Center. (2022). *Teens, Social Media and Technology 2022*. Pew Research Center.
The Runnymede Trust. (2020). *Lit in Colour*. The Runnymede Trust and Penguin Books UK.
The Runnymede Trust. (2020). *Teaching Migration, Belonging, and Empire in Secondary Schools*. The Runnymede Trust.

Podcasts

A Bit of Optimism – hosted by Simon Sinek
Diary of a CEO – hosted by Steven Bartlett
How to Fail – hosted by Elizabeth Day
Intersectionality Matters! – hosted by Kimberlé Crenshaw
Making the World Fairer – from Pearn Kandola
NASBTT Diversity in ITTE Podcast – hosted by Hannah Wilson and James Coleman
The School Should Be Podcast – hosted by Zahara Chowdhury.

Glossary

Allyship Actively supporting and advocating for marginalised groups, even when you don't share their identity or experiences. This includes speaking up against discrimination and examining your own biases.

Anti-racism Actively working to identify and challenge racism in all its forms, from individual prejudices to systemic inequalities. This goes beyond simply not being racist to taking action against racist practices and policies. To be anti-racist, we must understand that race is a social construct, not a biological fact, created to establish social hierarchies and systems of power and oppression.

Assimilation When members of marginalised groups feel pressured to adopt the dominant culture's behaviours, values and practices while suppressing their own cultural identity.

Belonging The feeling of being fully seen, accepted and valued as a member of a community. In schools, this means students feel they can authentically participate, contribute and thrive without hiding or changing who they are.

Cisgender When a person's gender identity aligns with the sex they were assigned at birth. For example, someone assigned female at birth who identifies as a woman is cisgender.

Code-switching When someone adapts their language, behaviour or appearance to fit different cultural contexts. Students might speak one way at home and another at school, which can be mentally exhausting.

Contracting The process of collaboratively establishing classroom expectations and boundaries with students. This creates shared ownership of classroom culture and helps students to feel invested in maintaining a safe learning environment.

Cultural capital The knowledge, behaviours and skills that can give students social and educational advantages. This includes familiarity with cultural references, language use and social norms that are often valued in educational settings.

Cultural competence/intelligence (CQ) The ability to understand, communicate and effectively interact with people across cultures. This includes awareness of our own cultural worldview, attitudes toward cultural differences, knowledge of different cultural practices and cross-cultural skills.

Curriculum audit A systematic review of teaching materials and practices to identify gaps, biases and areas for improvement in representation and inclusion.

Decolonising the curriculum Examining and revising teaching content and methods to include diverse perspectives and challenge dominant Western viewpoints. This includes questioning whose stories are told and whose voices are heard.

Deficit narrative Focusing on what students lack or can't do rather than their strengths and potential. This can particularly affect how we view and teach students from marginalised backgrounds.

Differentiation Adapting teaching methods and materials to meet the diverse needs of all students in a class. This goes beyond just making work easier or harder – it's about finding different ways to help each student succeed.

Digital exclusion Lack of access to digital devices, internet connection, or digital skills. This can create barriers to learning, especially when education relies increasingly on technology.

Digital literacy The ability to find, evaluate, create and communicate information using digital technologies. This includes understanding how to use technology safely and critically evaluate online information.

Disinformation False information that is deliberately created and shared to cause harm or achieve a specific goal. This is different from misinformation, which is false information shared without knowing it's false.

Diversity Different identities, experiences and perspectives within a group exist. In schools, this encompasses differences in race, ethnicity, gender, sexuality, disability, socioeconomic background, and other characteristics.

EAL (English as an Additional Language) Students who speak languages other than English at home or as their first language. This term focuses on the addition of English rather than treating other languages as a deficit.

Equity Ensuring fair access to opportunities by providing different levels of support based on individual needs rather than treating everyone exactly the same. In education, this means removing barriers that might prevent some students from fully participating and succeeding.

Gen Alpha People born between the mid-2010s and the early 2020s, the first generation to be born entirely in the twenty-first century.

Gender identity A person's internal sense of their own gender, which may or may not match the sex they were assigned at birth. This differs from gender expression (how someone presents their gender externally).

Gen Z People born between the mid to late 1990s and the early 2010s, also known as Zoomers.

Hedonic marking hypothesis The tendency to favour things that are easy to process or understand. In education, this can unconsciously influence how we respond to students' names or unfamiliar cultural practices.

Imposter syndrome Feeling like you don't belong or deserve your achievements, despite evidence of your capabilities. This can particularly affect students from underrepresented groups in certain spaces or subjects.

Inclusion Creating an environment where all students can fully participate and succeed. This goes beyond simply having diverse students present – it means actively ensuring everyone can meaningfully engage in all aspects of school life.

Intersectionality The way different aspects of a person's identity (like race, gender, class, disability) overlap and interact to shape their experiences, including experiences of discrimination or privilege. For example, a working-class Muslim girl might face different challenges from a middle-class Muslim boy. The term 'intersectionality' was coined by Kimberlé Crenshaw, an American civil rights advocate and a leading scholar of critical race theory.

LGBTQ+ An umbrella term for Lesbian, Gay, Bisexual, Transgender, Queer/Questioning, and other gender and sexual identities. The '+' acknowledges that there are many other identities within this community.

Lived experience The first-hand knowledge and perspectives that come from personally experiencing something. In education, recognising students' lived experiences means valuing the unique insights they bring from their own lives and backgrounds.

Manosphere An online subculture of websites and forums where men express frustration with gender relations, often promoting anti-feminist views and toxic masculinity. These spaces frequently feature misogynistic rhetoric that can negatively impact how men view relationships and gender equality.

Marginalised/minoritised communities Groups who have historically had less power or representation in society. The term 'minoritised' emphasises that this status comes from social and political processes rather than just numbers.

Masking When someone conceals aspects of their identity or personality to fit in with what they think is expected or acceptable. This can be particularly common among neurodivergent students or those from marginalised groups.

Microaggressions Subtle, often unintentional comments or actions that communicate hostile or negative attitudes toward marginalised groups. These can include things like mispronouncing names or making assumptions based on stereotypes.

Misinformation False or inaccurate information that is shared without knowing it's false. This is different from disinformation, which is false information that is deliberately created and shared to cause harm or achieve a specific goal.

Neurodiversity The natural variation in how human brains work, including differences in thinking, learning and processing information. This term recognises that neurological differences are normal variations rather than deficits.

Privilege Advantages that some people have simply because of their identity or background. These advantages are often invisible to those who have them. In schools, privilege might mean never having to worry if curriculum materials will reflect your culture or if you'll face discrimination.

Pronouns Words used to refer to people (she/her, he/him, they/them). Using someone's correct pronouns shows respect for their gender identity and creates an inclusive environment.

Psychological safety An environment where students feel safe to take risks, make mistakes and be themselves, without fear of negative consequences. This includes feeling able to ask questions, share opinions, and admit when they don't understand something.

Representation Seeing aspects of your identity reflected in curriculum materials, school staff and school culture. Good representation goes beyond token inclusion to show diverse people in non-stereotypical roles and situations.

Reverse mentoring When students mentor teachers or senior staff, particularly about their experiences as members of marginalised groups. This helps staff to better understand student perspectives and needs.

Safe space An environment where people can express themselves without fear of judgment, harassment or harm. In schools, this might be a physical space (like a classroom or club) or a general atmosphere that allows students to be themselves.

SEND (Special Educational Needs and Disabilities) A term covering a wide range of needs including physical disabilities, learning difficulties, and social, emotional or mental health needs. Students with SEND may need different types of support to fully access education.

Social anxiety Intense worry about social situations, particularly fear of judgment or negative evaluation by others. In the classroom, this might manifest as reluctance to participate in group work or present to the class.

Stereotype threat Feelings of angst and self-consciousness when a person is aware of a negative stereotype, bias or sentiment in relation to a group they belong to.

Tokenism Including a small number of people from marginalised groups to give the appearance of diversity without making meaningful changes to include their perspectives and needs.

Trauma-informed approach Understanding how traumatic experiences affect learning and behaviour, and adapting teaching practices to support affected students. This includes creating predictable routines and safe spaces.

Whataboutism Responding to concerns about one issue by bringing up a different issue, often to deflect or dismiss the original concern. For example, responding to concerns about racism by saying, 'But what about...'

Wise interventions Small but strategic changes in how we present information or structure activities that can have significant positive effects on student belonging and achievement.

Index